THE RELAXED AUTHOR

TAKE THE PRESSURE OFF YOUR ART
AND ENJOY THE CREATIVE JOURNEY

Joanna Penn & Mark Leslie Lefebvre

The Relaxed Author:
Take the Pressure Off Your Art and
Enjoy the Creative Journey

Copyright © Joanna Penn and Mark Leslie Lefebvre (2021)

All rights reserved. No part of this publication may be reproduced, stored in a retrieval system, or transmitted, in any form or by any means, without the prior written permission of the publisher.

ISBN Paperback: 978-1-913321-71-0
Large Print: 978-1-913321-73-4
Hardback: 978-1-913321-72-7

Published by Curl Up Press

Requests to publish work from this book should be sent to: joanna@TheCreativePenn.com

Cover and Interior Design: JD Smith

Printed by Lightning Source Ltd

www.CurlUpPress.com

Contents

Introduction   1
Why the 'relaxed' author?   5
You are not alone.
Why authors are NOT relaxed.   11

Part 1: Relaxed Writing   15

   1.1 Write what you love   17

   1.2 Write at your own pace   24

   1.3 Write in a series (if you want to)   32

   1.4 Schedule time to fill the creative well and for rest and relaxation   40

   1.5 Improve your writing process — but only if it fits with your lifestyle   45

Part 2: Relaxed Publishing   51

   2.1 Make empowered publishing choices that suit your personality and your life. Re-evaluate over time.   53

2.2	Understand persistence, patience and partnership if traditionally publishing	59
2.3	Value your work. You create intellectual property assets. Retain control as much as possible.	66
2.4	Publish at your own pace	73
2.5	Publish wide (or don't)	77
2.6	Sell direct to your audience	84
2.7	Don't let piracy and plagiarism derail you	93
2.8	Deal with cancel culture, bad reviews and haters	100
2.9	Find a community who support your publishing choices	111

Part 3: Relaxed Marketing — 117

3.1	Focus on the basics first	119
3.2	Simplify your author brand and website	128
3.3	Simplify and automate your email	136
3.4	Find one form of marketing that you enjoy and can sustain for the long term	143
3.5	Put book 1 in a series free or permafree and schedule regular promotions	154

3.6	Choose social media that suits you — or don't use it at all	159
3.7	Advertise in campaigns, not constantly	168
3.8	Outsource when you can	172
3.9	Embrace who you are. Double down on being human.	183
3.10	Think global, digital, long-term marketing	189

Part 4: Relaxed Business — 193

4.1	Do you really want to run an author business?	195
4.2	Create multiple streams of income	204
4.3	Eliminate tasks. Say 'no' more.	213
4.4	Organize and improve your processes	221
4.5	Use tools to make your process more efficient	227
4.6	Find voices you trust and tune out the rest	243
4.7	Learn about money	253
4.8	Look after your physical and mental health	258
4.9	Keep a long-term mindset	266

How to remain a relaxed author	273
Conclusion	279
Need more help?	281
Appendix 1: More reasons why authors are NOT relaxed	283
Appendix 2: More tips on how to be a relaxed author	293
Appendix 3: Resources by chapter	310
Appendix 4: Bibliography	326
More Books and Courses from Joanna Penn	331
More Books from Mark Leslie Lefebvre	335
About Joanna Penn	339
About Mark Leslie Lefebvre	341
Acknowledgments	343

Introduction

> "Believe that enjoying your work with all your heart is the only truly subversive position left to take as a creative person these days."
>
> Elizabeth Gilbert, *Big Magic*

There are so many books and tips on writing faster, marketing more, trying to hit the top of the charts, juicing algorithms, and hacking ads. These are all important things, and we have both talked about them ourselves and written books on related topics.

But we've also both been doing this long enough to see authors burning out and leaving the writing life because they turned what they love into a hamster wheel of ever more production and marketing tasks they hate.

It doesn't have to be this way.

In this book, we'll share our tips to help you become

a more relaxed author and quotes from other writers along the way.

Who are we?

Joanna Penn writes non-fiction for authors and is an award-nominated, New York Times and USA Today bestselling thriller author as J.F. Penn. She's also an award-winning podcaster, creative entrepreneur, and international professional speaker. Joanna left her corporate career a decade ago and now runs a multi-six-figure creative business based on her writing.

Mark Leslie Lefebvre is a multi-award-nominated writer who writes horror, urban fantasy, true ghost story books, and non-fiction for writers. He's a podcaster at Stark Reflections on Writing and Publishing, a professional speaker, and a publishing consultant at Draft2Digital. He has worked in the book industry since 1992, the same year his first short story was published.

We met online over a decade ago during the early days of the rise of self-publishing. We became friends in real life after meeting at author conferences and London Book Fair. Over the years, we have had discussions in public on stages and podcast interviews, as well as plenty of private chats over beer (Mark) and gin & tonic (Joanna).

We are both passionate about the indie author community and the empowerment of creatives to write the books they want — and make a living from their work. We also want to ensure it is a sustainable community full of happy, relaxed authors!

* * *

In this book, we have written separate sections in each chapter to retain our voices both on the page and in audio, as well as sharing tips from other writers. Each part covers a separate aspect of being an author — writing, publishing, marketing, and business.

There are resources to take your research further at the end of every chapter and you can download the appendices and more resources at:

TheCreativePenn.com/relaxedauthordownload

We hope you find the book useful on your way to becoming a more relaxed author.

* * *

Note from Joanna: There are affiliate links within this book to products and services that I recommend and use personally. This means that I receive a small percentage of the sale at no extra cost to you, and in some cases, you may receive a discount for using my link. I only recommend products and services that I believe are great for writers, so I hope you find them useful.

Why the 'relaxed' author?

Joanna: The definition of relaxed is "free from tension and anxiety," from the Latin *laxus*, meaning loose, and to be honest, I am not a relaxed or laid-back person in the broader sense.

Back in my teens, my nickname at school was Highly Stressed. I'm a Type A personality, driven by deadlines and achieving goals. I love to work and I burned out multiple times in my previous career as an IT consultant.

If we go away on a trip, I pack the schedule with back-to-back cultural things like museums and art galleries to help my book research. Or we go on adventure holidays with a clear goal, like cycling down the South-West coast of India. I can't even go for a long walk without training for another ultra-marathon!

So I am not a relaxed person — but I *am* a relaxed author.

If I wanted to spend most of my time doing something that made me miserable, I would go back to my old day job in consulting. I was paid well and worked fewer hours overall.

But I measure my life by what I create, and if I am not working on a creative project, I am not able to truly relax in my downtime. There are always more things I want to learn and write about, always more stories to be told and knowledge to share. I don't want to kill my writing life by over-stressing or burning out as an author.

I write what I love and follow my Muse into projects that feel right. I know how to publish and market books well enough to reach readers and make some money. I have many different income streams through my books, podcast and website.

Of course, I still have my creative and business challenges as well as mindset issues, just like any writer. That never goes away. But after a decade as a full-time author entrepreneur, I have a mature creative business and I've relaxed into the way I do things.

I love to write, but I also want a full and happy, healthy life. I'm still learning and improving as the industry shifts — and I change, too. I still have ambitious creative and financial goals, but I am going about them in a more relaxed way and in this book, I'll share some of my experiences and tips in the hope that you can discover your relaxed path, too.

* * *

Mark: One of the most fundamental things you can do in your writing life is look at how you want to spend your time. I think back to the concept of: 'You're often a reflection of the people you spend the most time with.' Therefore, typically, your best friend, or perhaps your partner, is often a person you love spending time with. Because there's something inherently special about spending time with this person who resonates in a meaningful way, and you feel more yourself because you're with them.

In many ways, writing, or the path that you are on as a writer, is almost like being on a journey with an invisible partner. You are you. But you are also the writer you. And there's the two of you traveling down the road of life together. And so that same question arises. What kind of writer-self do you want to spend all your time with?

Do you want to spend all your time with a partner that is constantly stressed out or constantly trying to reach deadlines based on somebody else's prescription of what success is?

Or would you rather spend time with a partner who pauses to take a contemplative look at your own life, your own comfort, your own passion and the things that you are willing to commit to? Someone who allows that all to happen in a way that feels natural and comfortable to you.

I'm a fan of the latter, of course, because then you can focus on the things you're passionate about and the things you're hopeful about rather than the things you're fearful about and those that bring anxiety and stress into your life.

To me, that's part of being a relaxed author. That underlying acceptance before you start to plan things out.

If the writing life is a marathon, not a sprint, then pacing, not rushing, may be the key.

We have both seen burnout in the author community. People who have pushed themselves too hard and just couldn't keep up with the impossible pace they set for themselves. At times, indie authors would wear that stress, that anxiety, that rush to produce more and more, as a badge of honor. It's fine to be proud of the hard work that you do. It's fine to be proud of pushing yourself to always do better, and be better. But when you push too far — beyond your limits — you can ultimately do yourself more harm than good.

Everyone has their own unique pace—something that they are comfortable with—and one key is to experiment until you find that pace, and you can settle in for the long run.

There's no looking over your shoulder at the other writers. There's no panicking about the ones outpacing you.

You're in this with yourself.

And, of course, with those readers who are anticipating those clearly communicated milestones of your releases.

I think that what we both want for authors is to see them reaching those milestones at their own paces, in their own comfort, delighting in the fact their readers are there cheering them on.

Because we'll be silently cheering them along as well, knowing that they've set a pace, making relaxed author lifestyle choices, that will benefit them in the long run.

* * *

"I'm glad you're writing this book. I know I'm not the only author who wants peace, moments of joy, and to enjoy the journey. Indie publishing is a luxury that I remember not having, I don't want to lose my sense of gratitude."

Anonymous author from our survey

You are not alone. Why authors are NOT relaxed.

In June 2021 we sent out a survey related to this book. Thanks to the 200 authors who contributed with what stresses them out and how they manage.

Here are just some of the reasons that authors are not relaxed:

- Overwhelm. The To Do list never ends with all the writing, publishing, and marketing tasks.

- Finding time to write and feeling like I just can't balance everything I need to do with writing and with life.

- I can't write fast enough to make enough books to make enough money.

- There's always more to learn, and it's hard to be satisfied with where you are now.

- Comparing myself to other writers and imposter syndrome. There is always someone more successful financially. There is always a book that is better than mine. My craft will never be good enough.

- Writer's block.

- Worrying about getting the right agent, or whether I will get one at all, and then whether I get a publishing deal that's worthwhile. What happens if I never get a deal, or I do get one, but the book flops and the publisher and my agent dump me? If I have to start all over again, is it even worth it?

- Social media. What do I post? What about negative or nasty comments?

- Paid ads. I've learned how to do them so why don't they work? They take up too much time and too much money.

- Spreadsheets and data and granular tracking that suck all the fun from writing.

- Writing sales descriptions (also known as blurbs). Why is it harder to write a paragraph than a whole book?

- Money. Spending too much on creating the books without making a return. Constant balance between spending to grow and living costs, as well as worry about my financial future.

- People stealing my hard work — pirates, plagiarism, Hollywood. There seem to be people at every turn who want to fleece writers.

- What do I put in regular emails to readers? Plus, I don't have time to interact with readers, anyway.

- Managing my time between writing and everything else — including time with my family.

- Waiting for other people (editors, beta readers, etc.) to meet deadlines and the fear that if they miss them, I will miss my preorder, or publication deadline.

- Fear of judgment. What will people think of me? Why does this bad review make me so miserable?

- Feeling like a failure as I am just not selling as many books as I would like, or as many as other people seem to be.

- Legal things. What if I sign a bad contract? What if I accidentally break data protection laws? What if I get sued? How do I protect myself?

- Criticism from people I care about — my partner, my family, my friends. I wonder whether I should bother even writing?

- I don't know who to listen to. Everyone has different opinions about what works in terms of publishing and marketing. How do I know what will work for me?

- Formatting and getting everything to look right. It is so finickity.

- The power that the biggest publishing and technology companies have over an author's career and the lack of control if they decide something is wrong with your book.

- Health issues. What happens if I can't write anymore?

- The pace of change. Technology is moving fast. How am I meant to keep up with everything?

- Uncertainty. Not knowing how the book/s will do and what kind of success I might have, or whether it will all just be for nothing.

If you feel any/or all of the above, then you are not alone! We hope this book will go some way to alleviating the stress as we go through the topics in more detail in the chapters ahead.

Part 1: Relaxed Writing

1.1 Write what you love

Joanna: The pandemic has taught us that life really is short. *Memento mori* — remember, you will die.

What is the point of spending precious time writing books you don't want to write?

If we only have a limited amount of time and only have a limited number of books that we can write in a lifetime, then we need to choose to write the books that we love. If I wanted a job doing something I don't enjoy, then I would have remained in my stressful old career as an IT consultant — when I certainly wasn't relaxed!

Taking that further, if you try to write things you don't love, then you're going to have to read what you don't love as well, which will take more time. I love writing thrillers because that's what I love to read. Back when I was miserable in my day job as an IT consultant, I would go to the bookstore at lunchtime and buy thrillers. I would read them on the train to and from work and during the lunch break. Anything for a few minutes of escape. That's the same feeling I try to give my readers now.

I know the genre inside and out. If I had to write something else, I would have to read and learn that other genre and spend time doing things I don't love. In fact, I don't even know how you *can* read things you don't enjoy. I only give books a few pages and if they don't resonate, I stop reading. Life really is too short.

You also need to run your own race and travel your own journey. If you try to write in a genre you are not immersed in, you will always be looking sideways at what other authors are doing, and that can cause comparisonitis — when you compare yourself to others, most often in an unfavorable way. Definitely not relaxing!

Writing something you love has many intrinsic rewards other than sales.

Writing is a career for many of us, but it's a passion first, and you don't want to feel like you've wasted your time on words you don't care about.

"Write what you know" is terrible advice for a long-term career as at some point, you will run out of what you know. It should be "write what you want to learn about." When I want to learn about a topic, I write a book on it because that feeds my curiosity and I love book research, it's how I enjoy spending my time, especially when I travel, which is also part of how I relax.

If you write what you love and make it part of your lifestyle, you will be a far more relaxed author.

* * *

Mark: It's common that writers are drawn into storytelling from some combination of passion, curiosity, and unrelenting interest. We probably read or saw something that inspired us, and we wanted to express those ideas or the resulting perspectives that percolated in our hearts and minds. Or we read something and thought, "Wow, I could do this; but I would have come at it differently or I would approach the situation or subject matter with my own flair."

So, we get into writing with passion and desire for storytelling. And then sometimes along the way, we recognize the critical value of having to become an entrepreneur, to understand the business of writing and publishing. And part of understanding that aspect of being an author is writing to market, and understanding shifts and trends in the industry, and adjusting to those ebbs and flows of the tide. But sometimes, we lose sight of the passion that drew us to writing in the first place. And so, writing the things that you love can be a beacon to keep you on course.

I love the concept of "Do something that you love, and you'll never work a day in your life." And that's true in some regard because I've always felt that way for almost my entire adult life. I've been very lucky. But at the same time, I work extremely hard at what I love.

Some days are harder than others, and some things are really difficult, frustrating and challenging; but **at the end of the day, I have the feeling of satisfaction that I spent my time doing something I believe in**.

I've been a bookseller my entire life even though I don't sell books in brick-and-mortar bookstores anymore—that act of physically putting books in people's hands. But to this day, what I do is virtually putting books in people's hands, both as an author and as an industry representative who is passionate about the book business.

I was drawn to that world via my passion for writing. And that's what continues to compel me forward. I tried to leave the corporate world to write full time in 2018 but realized there was an intrinsic satisfaction to working in that realm, to embracing and sharing my insights and knowledge from that arena to help other writers. And I couldn't give that up.

For me, the whole core, the whole essence of why I get up in the morning has to do with storytelling, creative inspiration, and wanting to inspire and inform other people to be the best that they can be in the business of writing and publishing.

And that's what keeps me going when the days are hard.

Passion as the inspiration to keep going

There are always going to be days that aren't easy.

There will be unexpected barriers that hit you as a writer.

You'll face that mid-novel slump or realize that you have to scrap an entire scene or even plotline, and feel like going back and re-starting is just too much.

You might find the research required to be overwhelming or too difficult.

There'll be days when the words don't flow, or the inspiration that initially struck you seems to have abandoned you for greener pastures.

Whatever it is, some unexpected frustration can create what can appear to be an insurmountable block.

And, when that happens, if it's a project you don't love, you're more likely to let those barriers get in your way and stop you.

But if it's a project that you're passionate about, and you're writing what you love, that alone can be what greases the wheels and helps reduce that friction to keep you going.

At the end of the day, writing what you love can be a honing, grounding, and centering beacon that allows you to want to wake up in the morning and enjoy the process as much as possible even when the hard work comes along.

* * *

"For me, relaxation comes from writing what I know and love and trusting the emergent process. As a discovery writer, I experience great joy when the story, characters and dialogue simply emerge in their own time and their own way. It feels wonderful."

Valerie Andrews

"Writing makes me a relaxed author. Just getting lost in a story of my own creation, discovering new places and learning what makes my characters tick is the best way I know of relaxing. Even the tricky parts, when I have no idea where I am going next, have a special kind of charm."

Imogen Clark

1.2 Write at your own pace

Mark: Writing at your own pace will help you be a more relaxed author because you're not stressing out by trying to keep up with someone else. Of course, we all struggle with comparing ourselves to others.

Take a quick look around and you can always find someone who has written more books than you. Nora Roberts, traditionally published author, writes a book a month. Lindsey Buroker, fantasy indie author, writes a book a month of over 100,000 words.

If you compare yourself to someone else and you try to write at their pace, that is not going to be **your** relaxed schedule.

On the other hand, if you compare yourself to Donna Tartt, who writes one book every decade, you might feel like some speed-demon crushing that word count and mastering rapid release.

Looking at what others are doing could result in you thinking you're really slow or you could think that you're super-fast.

What does that kind of comparison actually get you?

I remember going to see a talk by Canadian literary author Farley Mowat when I was a young budding writer. I'll never forget one thing he said from that stage: "Any book that takes you less than four years to write is not a real book."

Young teenage Mark was devastated, hurt and disappointed to hear him say that because my favorite author at the time, Piers Anthony, was writing and publishing two to three novels a year. I loved his stuff, and his fantasy and science fiction had been an important inspiration in my writing at that time. (The personal notes I add to the end of my stories and novels came from enjoying his so much).

That focus on there being only a single way, a single pace to write, ended up preventing me from enjoying the books I had already been loving because I was doing that comparisonitis Joanna talks about, but as a reader.

I took someone else's perspective too much to heart and I let that ruin a good thing that had brought me personal joy and pleasure.

It works the same way as a writer. Because we have

likely developed a pattern, or a way that works for us that is our own.

We all have a pace that we comfortably walk; a way we prefer to drive. A pattern or style of how and when and what we prefer to eat. We all have our own unique comfort food.

There are these patterns that we're comfortable with, and potentially because they are natural to us. If you try to force yourself to write at a pace that's not natural to you, things can go south in your writing and your mental health.

And I'm not suggesting any particular pace, except for the one that's most natural and comfortable to you.

If writing fast is something that you're passionate about, and you're good at it, and it's something you naturally do, why would you stop yourself from doing that? Just like if you're a slow writer and you're trying to write fast: why are you doing that to yourself?

There's a common pop song line used by numerous bands over the years that exhorts you to "shake what you got." I like to think the same thing applies here. And do it with pride and conviction. Because what you got is unique and awesome. Own it, and shake it with pride.

You have a way you write and a word count per writing session that works for you.

And along with that, you likely know what time you can assign to writing because of other commitments like family time, leisure time, and work (assuming you're not a full-time writer). Simple math can provide you with a way to determine how long it will take to get your first draft written. So, your path and plans are clear. And you simply take the approach that aligns with your writer DNA.

Understanding what that pace is for **you** helps alleviate an incredible amount of stress that you do not need to thrust upon yourself. Because if you're not going to be able to enjoy it while you're doing it, what's the point?

Your pace might change project to project

While your pace can change over time, your pace can also change project to project. And sometimes the time actually spent writing can be a smaller portion of the larger work involved.

I was on a panel at a conference once and someone asked me how long it took to write my non-fiction book of ghost stories, *Haunted Hamilton*.

"About four days," I responded.

And while that's true — I crafted the first draft over four long and exhausting days writing as much as sixteen hours each day — the reality was I had been doing research for months. But the pen didn't actually hit the paper until just a few days before my deadline to turn the book over to my editor.

That was for a non-fiction book; but I've found I do similar things with fiction. I noodle over concepts and ideas for months before I actually commit words to the page.

The reason this comes to mind is that I think it's important to recognize the way that I write is I first spend a lot of time in my head to understand and chew on things. And then by the time it comes to actually getting the words onto the paper, I've already done much of the pre-writing mentally.

It's sometimes not fair when you're comparing yourself to someone else to look at how long they physically spend in front of a keyboard hammering on that word count, because they might have spent a significantly longer amount of a longer time either outlining or conceptualizing the story in their mind or in their heart before they sat down to write. So that's part of the pace, too. Because sometimes, if we only look at the time spent at the 'writer's desk,' we fool ourselves when we think that we're a slow writer or a fast writer.

* * *

Joanna:

Your pace will change over your career

My first novel took 14 months and now I can write a first draft in about six weeks because I have more experience. It's also more relaxing for me to write a book now than it was in the beginning, because I didn't know what I was doing back then.

Your pace will change per project

I have a non-fiction work in progress, my *Shadow Book* (working title), which I have started several times. I have about 30,000 words but as I write this, I have backed away from it because I'm (still) not ready. There's a lot more research and thinking I need to do. Similarly, some people take years writing a memoir or a book with such emotional or personal depth that it needs more to bring it to life.

Your pace will also shift depending on where you are in the arc of life

Perhaps you have young kids right now, or you have a health issue, or you're caring for someone who is ill. Perhaps you have a demanding day job so you have less time to write. Perhaps you really need extended time away from writing, or just a holiday. Or maybe there's a global pandemic and frankly, you're too stressed to write!

The key to pacing in a book is variability — and that's true of life, too. Write at the pace that works for you and don't be afraid to change it as you need to over time.

* * *

"I think the biggest thing for me is reminding myself that I'm in this to write. Sometimes I can get caught up in all the moving pieces of editing and publishing and marketing, but the longer I go without writing, or only writing because I have to get the next thing done instead of for enjoyment, the more stressed and anxious I become. But if I make time to fit in what I truly love, which is the process of writing without putting pressure on myself to meet a deadline, or to be perfect, or to meet somebody else's expectations — that's when I become truly relaxed."

Ariele Sieling

1.3 Write in a series (if you want to)

Joanna: I have some stand-alone books but most of them are in series, both for non-fiction and for my fiction as J.F. Penn. It's how I like to read and write.

As we draft this book, I'm also writing book 12 in my ARKANE series, *Tomb of Relics*. It's relaxing because **I know my characters, I know my world; I know the structure of how an ARKANE story goes.** I know what to put in it to please my readers. I have already done the work to set up the series world and the main characters and now all I need is a plot and an antagonist.

It's also quicker to write and edit because I've done it before. Of course, you need to put in the work initially so the series comes together, but once you've set that all up, each subsequent book is easier.

You can also be more relaxed because **you already have an audience** who will (hopefully) buy the book because they bought the others. You will know approximately how many sales you'll get on launch and there will be people ready to review.

Writing in a non-fiction series is also a really good

idea because you know your audience and you can offer them more books, products and services that will help them within a niche. While they might not be sequential, they should be around the same topic, for example, this is part of my Books for Authors series.

Financially, it makes sense to have a series as you will **earn more revenue per customer** as they will (hopefully) buy more than one book. It's also easier and more relaxing to market as you can set one book to free or a limited time discount and drive sales through to other books in the series.

Essentially, writing a book in a series makes it easier to fulfill both creative and financial goals. However, if you love to read and write stand-alone books, and some genres suit stand-alones better than series anyway, then, of course, go with what works for you!

* * *

Mark: I like to equate this to no matter where you travel in the world, if you find a McDonald's you pretty much know what's on the menu and you know what to expect.

When you write in a series, it's like returning to hang out with old friends.

You know their backstory; you know their history so you can easily fall into a new conversation about something and not have to get caught up on understanding what you have in common. So that's an enormous benefit of relaxing into something like, "Oh, I'm sitting down over coffee, chatting with some old friends. They're telling me a new story about something that happened to them. I know who they are, I know what they're made out of." And this new plot, this new situation, they may have new goals, they may have new ways they're going to grow as characters, but they're still the same people that we know and love.

And that's a huge benefit that I only discovered recently because I'm only right now working on book four in my Canadian Werewolf series.

Prior to that, I had three different novels that were all the first book in a series with no book two. And it was stressful for me. Writing anything seemed to take forever.

I was causing myself anxiety by jumping around and writing new works as opposed to realizing I could go visit a locale I'm familiar and comfortable with. And I can see new things in the same locale just like sometimes you can see new things and people you know and love already, especially when you introduce something new into the world and you see how they react to it. For me, there's nothing more wonderful than that sort of homecoming. It's like a nostalgic feeling when you do that.

I've seen a repeated pattern where writers spend years writing their first book. I started *A Canadian Werewolf in New York* in 2006 and I did not publish it until ten years later, after finishing it in 2015. (FYI, that wasn't my first novel. I had written three and published one of them prior to that).

That first novel can take so long because you're learning.

You're learning about your characters, about the craft, about the practice of writing, about the processes that you're testing along the way. And if you are working on your first book and it's taking longer than planned, please don't beat yourself up for that. It's a process. Sometimes that process takes more time.

I sometimes wonder if this is related to our perception of time as we age. When you're 10 years old, a day compared to your lifetime is a significant amount of time, and thinking about a year later is considering a time that is one-tenth of your life. When you have a few more decades or more under your belt, that year is a smaller part of the whole. If you're 30, a year is only one-thirtieth of your life. A much smaller piece.

Just having written more books, particularly in a series, removes the pressure of that one book to represent all of you as a writer.

I had initial anxiety at writing the second book in my Canadian Werewolf series. Book two was more terrifying in some ways than book one because finally, after all this time, I had something good that I didn't want to ruin. Should I leave well enough alone?

But I was asked to write a short story to a theme in an anthology, and using my main character from that first novel allowed me to discover I could have fun spending more time with these characters and this world.

And I also realized that people wanted to read more about these characters. I didn't just want to write about them, but other people wanted to read about them too. And that makes the process so much easier to keep going with them.

So one of the other benefits that helps to relax me as a writer working on a series is I have a better understanding of who my audience is, and who my readers are, and who will want this, and who will appreciate it. So I know what worked, I know what resonated with them, and I know I can give them that next thing. I have discovered that **writing in a series is a far more relaxed way of understanding your target audience better**. Because it's not just a single shot in the dark, it's a consistent on-going stream.

Let me reflect on a bit of a caveat, because I'm not suggesting sticking to only a single series or universe. As writers, we have plenty of ideas and inspirations, and it's okay to embrace some of the other ones that come to us.

When I think about the Canadian rock trio, Rush, a band that produced 19 studio albums and toured for 40 years, I acknowledge a very consistent band over the decades. And yet, they weren't the same band that they were when they started playing together, even though it was the same three guys since Neil Peart joined Geddy Lee and Alex Lifeson. They changed what they wrote about, what they sang about, themes, styles, approaches to making music, all of this. They adapted and changed their style at least a dozen times over the course of their career. No album was exactly like the previous album, and they experimented, and they tried things. But there was a consistency of the audience that went along with them. And as writers, we can potentially have that same thing where we know there are going to be people who will follow us. Think about Stephen King, a writer who has been writing in many different subjects and genres. And yet there's a core group of people who will enjoy everything he writes, and he has that Constant Reader he always keeps in mind.

And so, when we write in a series, we're thinking about that constant reader in a more relaxed way because that constant reader, like our characters, like our worlds, like our universes, is like we're just returning to a comfortable, cozy spot where we're just going to hang out with some good friends for a bit. Or, as the contemplative Rush song *Time Stand Still* expresses, the simple comfort and desire of spending some quality time having a drink with a friend.

Resources:

- Interview with fantasy author Lindsay Buroker on writing a series — www.TheCreativePenn.com/writeseries
- *How to Write a Series* — Sara Rosett

1.4 Schedule time to fill the creative well and for rest and relaxation

Mark: What we do as writers is quite cerebral, so **we need to give ourselves mental breaks** in the same way we need to sleep regularly.

Our bodies require sleep. And it's not just physical rest for our bodies to regenerate, it's for our minds to regenerate. We need that to stay sane, to stay alive, to stay healthy.

The reality for us as creatives is that we're writing all the time, whether or not we're in front of a keyboard or have a pen in our hand. We're always writing, continually sucking the marrow from the things that are happening around us, even when we're not consciously aware of it. And sometimes when we are more consciously aware of it, that awareness can feel forced. It can feel stressful. When you give yourself the time to just let go, to just relax, wonderful things can happen. And they can come naturally, never feeling that urgent sense of pressure.

Downtime, for me, is making space for those magic moments to happen.

I was recently listening to Episode 556 of The Creative Penn podcast where Joanna talked about the serendipity of those moments when you're traveling and you're going to a museum and you see something. And you're not consciously there to research for a book, but you see something that just makes a connection for you. And you would not have had that for your writing had you not given yourself the time to just be doing and enjoying something else.

And so, whenever I need to resolve an issue or a problem in a project I'm writing, which can cause stress, I will do other things. I will go for a run or walk the dogs, wash the dishes or clean the house. Or I'll put on some music and sing and dance like nobody is watching or listening—and thank goodness for that, because that might cause *them* needless anxiety. The key is, I will do something different that allows my mind to just let go. And somewhere in the subconscious, usually the answer comes to me. **Those non-cerebral activities can be very restorative.**

Yesterday, my partner Liz and I met her daughter at the park. And while we quietly waited, the two of us wordlessly enjoyed the sights and sounds of people walking by, the river in the background, the wind blowing through the leaves in the trees above us. That moment wasn't a purposeful, "Hey, we're going to chill and relax." But we found about five minutes of restorative calm in the day.

A brief, but powerful 'Ah' moment.

And when I got back to writing this morning, I drew upon some of the imagery from those few minutes. I didn't realize at the time I was experiencing the moment yesterday that I was going to incorporate some of that imagery in today's writing session. And that's the serendipity that just flows very naturally in those scheduled and even unscheduled moments of relaxation.

* * *

Joanna: I separate this into two aspects because I'm good at one and terrible at the other!

I schedule time to fill the creative well as often as possible. This is something that Julia Cameron advises in *The Artist's Way*, and I find it an essential part of my creative practice. Essentially, you can't create from an empty mind. **You have to actively seek out ways to spark ideas.**

International travel is a huge part of my fiction inspiration, in particular. This has been impossible during the pandemic and has definitely impacted my writing. I also go to exhibitions and art galleries, as well as read books, watch films and documentaries.

If I don't fill my creative well, then I feel empty, like I will never have another idea, that perhaps my writing life is over. Some people call that writer's block but I know that feeling now. It just means I haven't filled my creative well and I need to schedule time to do that so I can create again.

Consume and produce. That's the balance you need in order to keep the creative well filled and the words flowing.

In terms of scheduling time to relax instead of doing book research, I find this difficult because I love to work. My husband says that I'm like a little sports car that goes really, really fast and doesn't stop until it hits a wall. I operate at a high productivity level and then I crash!

But the restrictions of the pandemic have helped me learn more about relaxation, after much initial frustration. I have walked in nature and lain in the garden in the hammock and recently, we went to the seaside for the first time in 18 months. I lay on the stones and watched the waves. I was the most relaxed I've been in a long time.

I didn't look at my phone. I wasn't listening to a podcast or an audiobook. We weren't talking. We were just being there in nature and relaxing.

Authors are always thinking and feeling because everything feeds our work somehow. But we have to have both aspects — active time to fill the creative well and passive time to rest and relax.

**

"I go for lots of walks and hikes in
the woods. These help me work out the
kinks in my plots, and also to feel more relaxed!
(Exercise is an added benefit!)"

T.W. Piperbrook

Resources:

- The Ultimate Guide to Creative Rest for Indie Authors — www.selfpublishingadvice.org/the-ultimate-guide-to-creative-rest-for-indie-authors

1.5 Improve your writing process — but only if it fits with your lifestyle

Joanna: A lot of stress can occur in writing if we try to change or improve our process too far beyond our natural way of doing things.

For example, trying to be a detailed plotter with a spreadsheet when you're really a discovery writer, or trying to dictate 5,000 words per hour when you find it easier to hand write slowly into a journal.

Productivity tips from other writers can really help you tweak your personal process, but only if they work for you — and I say this as someone who has a book on *Productivity for Authors*!

Of course, it's a good idea to improve things, but once you try something, analyze whether it works for you — either with data or just how you feel. If it works, great. Adopt it into your process. If it doesn't work, then discard it.

For example, I wrote my first novel in Microsoft Word. When I discovered Scrivener, I changed my process and never looked back because it made my life so much easier. I don't write in order and

Scrivener made it easier to move things around.

I also discovered that it was easier for me to get into my first draft writing and creating when I was away from the desk I use for business, podcasting, and marketing tasks. I started to write in a local cafe and later on in a co-working space. During the pandemic lockdown, I used specific playlists to create a form of separation as I couldn't physically go somewhere else.

Editing is an important part of the writing process but you have to find what works for you, which will also change over time. Some are authors are more relaxed with a messy first draft, then rounds of rewrites while working with multiple editors. Others do one careful draft and then use a proof-reader to check the finished book. There are as many ways to write as there are writers.

A relaxed author chooses the process that works in the most effective way for them and makes the book the best it can be.

* * *

Mark: When it comes to process, there are times when you're doing something that feels natural, versus times when you're learning a new skill.

Consciously and purposefully learning new skills can be stressful; particularly because it's something we often put so much emphasis or importance upon.

But when you adapt on-going learning as a normal part of your life, a natural part of who and what you are, that stress can flow away. I'm always about learning new skills; but over time I've learned how to absorb learning into my everyday processes.

I'm a pantser, or discovery writer, or whatever term we can apply that makes us feel better about it. And every time I've tried to stringently outline a book, it has been a stressful experience and I've not been satisfied with the process or the result.

Perhaps I satisfied the part of me that thought I wanted to be more like other writers, but I didn't satisfy the creative person in me. I was denying that flow that has worked for me.

I did, of course, naturally introduce a few new learnings into my attempts to outline; so I stuck with those elements that worked, and abandoned the elements that weren't working, or were causing me stress.

The thought of self-improvement often comes with images of blood, sweat, and tears. It doesn't have to. You don't have to bleed to do this; it can be something that you do at your own pace. You can do it in a way that you're comfortable with so it's causing you no stress, but allowing you to learn and grow and improve. And if it doesn't work but you force yourself to keep doing it because a famous writer or a six-figure author said, "this is the way to do it," you create pressure. And when you don't do it that way, you can think of yourself as a failure as opposed to thinking of it as, "No, this is just the way that I do things."

When you accept how you do things, if they result in effectively getting things done and feeling good about it at the same time, you have less resistance, you have less friction, you have less tension.

Constantly learning, adapting, and evolving is good. But forcing ourselves to try to be or do something that we are not or that doesn't work for us, that causes needless anxiety.

* * *

"I think a large part of it comes down to reminding myself WHY I write. This can mean looking back at positive reviews, so I can see how much joy others get from my writing, or even just writing something brand new for the sake of exploring an idea. Writing something just for me, rather than for an audience, reminds me how much I enjoy writing, which helps me to unwind a bit and approach my projects with more playfulness."

Icy Sedgwick

Part 2: Relaxed Publishing

2.1 Make empowered publishing choices that suit your personality and your life. Re-evaluate over time.

First of all, it's important to note that this is not a book on how to publish. We both have books, podcast episodes, and free online resources listed below, so this section is more about how to be relaxed about your publishing choices.

Mark: For every book, I **look at the intended audience and the intended outcome**. Each book has its own goal.

Sometimes the goal is to sell print books versus ebooks. Typically, if I want to sell a lot of print books or I want to see the book in bookstores because I know that the book is more of a souvenir experience for the reader, I'll start with offering the book to traditional publishers.

I know that route typically means I won't make as much money, but I *will* reach readers I wouldn't normally reach through print-on-demand self-publishing. This works nicely for regionally themed books, such as my books about local ghosts. My publisher can, and has been able to, get those types of books into local and chain bookstores, Costco, and Walmart. (Admittedly, I made decent income off one of my books that had a full skid available in a Costco in Sudbury, Ontario. But that was because of a significant volume of sales.)

If I wanted to reach a global digital audience, there's nothing better than indie publishing the book myself and making it available wide. My book can be available in virtually every country around the world.

So when I'm deciding on the publishing path for a book, I consider where and how, the format I want to move the most copies in, and the importance of the margin percentage I will earn.

There is a bit of a gray area in between traditional publishing and indie publishing, because I have definitely sold a lot more self-published books in print than I've sold traditionally published titles in ebook format.

But that's the basic perspective I take. Because if you have an idea of the strengths and weaknesses of the different options, you can make informed choices.

Plans and goals are tools, not restraints

It's important to remember that if you empower yourself with a publishing plan or goal, you're not locked into that. Unless you sign contracts with deadlines and commitments, you can alter those plans should the need arise. It's often relaxing to know that.

Self-evaluating your goals and plans over time is so critical. We may take the time to plan things out, but we don't take the time to accept the fact that the plans can change, and that our goals may change, and that our desires may change, and that the entire project may change. It's crucial that we allow ourselves that flexibility.

* * *

Joanna: Choosing a certain publishing path will have an impact on your wider life, so it's important to understand which choices might enable you to be more relaxed.

For example, if you want other people to manage all the aspects of publishing the book and provide some help around marketing, then you might be more relaxed with traditional publishing. Others find the lack of creative control frustrating and choose to go independent as it allows them more freedom.

If you go the independent route and choose to put your book/s into KDP Select, you'll be part of a community who publish fast and regularly. This might be relaxing in some ways as you only have to consider one retailer, but you might also find yourself on a content creation hamster wheel that stresses you out.

If you choose to go wide, it might be more relaxing to spread your risk and reward across retailers but it might also be stressful as you have to update multiple stores and do different kinds of marketing.

You can also cause yourself stress around contractual obligations and timing. If you choose to traditionally publish, your publisher might have an aggressive publishing schedule or you might sign a contract with a deadline date for delivery. If something happens in your life, you could end up being more stressed than if you had published it yourself at your own pace.

Indie authors can stress themselves out in a similar way by setting aggressive pre-order dates or using crowdfunding platforms with immoveable timelines.

The important thing is to know yourself well enough to make choices that suit your personality and your life.

I like control and the freedom to change how I work and when I publish, so I love being an independent author. I think globally and I like multiple streams of income, so I publish wide with my main author brands in English, although I use KU for my books in German and my mum's sweet romance under Penny Appleton, as I don't have the ability to market those books in other ways.

The relaxed author choice is not about indie vs. traditional publishing, or KU vs. wide. It can be achieved however you publish, but only if you choose what's best for your personality and lifestyle.

Resources:

- *Successful Self-Publishing: How to Self-Publish and Market Your Book* — Joanna Penn
- *Wide for the Win: Strategies to Sell Globally via Multiple Platforms and For Your Own Path to Success* — Mark Leslie Lefebvre
- *Killing it on Kobo: Leverage Insights to Optimize Publishing and Marketing Strategies: Grow Your Global Sales and Increase Revenue on Kobo* — Mark Leslie Lefebvre

2.2 Understand persistence, patience and partnership if traditionally publishing

Mark: If you decide to get involved in traditional publishing, you'll need to apply additional helpings of a few of the elements of what I call *The 7 P's of Publishing Success*: Persistence, Patience, and Partnership.

You'll have to be extremely persistent and patient within the submission process and also have to deal with the reality of rejection.

Excellent books get rejected every single day because there's only so much time and space for a publisher to deal with the onslaught of submissions. They publish a tiny percentage of all proposals and manuscripts they receive. It can take years to lock in a publishing deal and see that book in print.

Within traditional publishing, there is a lot more collaboration and handing off of responsibilities, not to mention reliance on other people. On one hand, someone else is paying for the editing and design, and layout, and handling the logistics of publishing. And they're also paying you.

Ideally, you're receiving an advance that's often paid out in three parts. The first upon signing of the contract; the second upon delivery of the manuscript; the third upon publication. That money flowing in your direction and the costs being handled by your publisher can reduce financial anxiety for you.

But on the flip-side, be aware of the following potential cause of anxiety. You may, or may not have control over the cover design, the sales/back cover copy on the book, the release date, and other factors.

With the largest publisher I work with, I see royalty statements and a royalty check once per year, and have no real visibility into how my books are selling. It's quite the opposite of logging into your direct sales dashboard and hitting the refresh button to see how your books are selling today so far.

For some authors, removing the temptation of looking at the sales dashboard instead of doing something productive in your writing or brand-building can be a glorious thing. For me, it forces me to take a long-term viewpoint when it comes to writing and marketing. And, interestingly, that causes me far less stress. That ends up leaking over into my self-publishing self, who spends less time fixated on my current ranking or daily sales dashboards.

Consider where and what causes you the least amount of anxiety and stress before contemplating this option. Traditional publishing can take years to see through a single book project. While the money does flow in the right direction and isn't coming out of my own pocket, it's definitely less money per unit sale, and it doesn't come on a more rapid monthly basis.

Choosing not to decide is still making a choice

For me, embracing both traditional publishing and self-publishing has allowed me to expand my revenue streams, my author brand reach, and my reliance on any single major source of income. It has allowed me to be more relaxed.

Fellow Canadian horror author Steve Vernon comes to mind as someone else who has embraced this type of publishing. Most traditional publishers will release a single book a year with any author. They are often tied to a four-season selling cycle of a publisher selling to a bookstore chain buyer in New York, Toronto, or London.

But Steve is very prolific. He not only works with multiple publishers — because no single traditional publisher could keep up with his production output — but he also indie publishes other books.

It would be stressful for Steve to write and produce less. So embracing both worlds offers him the best of all possible worlds.

Another example is my good friend Kevin J. Anderson. Kevin, who has published more than 170 books, and has over 23 million copies in print in thirty languages, releases anywhere between four to eight books a year. He works with multiple publishers and multiple collaborators, and also indie publishes numerous titles. His decades of insight into traditional publishing allow him the ability to split and optimize the rights he licenses to publishers by format and geography and maximize the potential for income.

For Kevin, like for Steve, both born dynamic storytellers through-and-through, writing and publishing less would likely be far more stressful.

A contract is a negotiation

One important thing to remember about traditional publishing is that if a publisher offers you a contract, it's part of a negotiation. You don't need to accept it. And you can request revisions. I learned plenty of strategies over the years for clauses to look for and avoid via books and blog articles from Kristine Kathryn Rusch, as well as detailed contract seminars from Eric Flint at Superstars Writing Seminars conferences.

If a publisher sends a contract, that's their offer. And it's often a boilerplate template they send to everyone attempting to grab as many rights as possible. **You can request changes**, ask for different compensation, and request to strike specific clauses.

Important considerations are:

- What formats does the author still hold the rights to?
- Which territories is this contract for?
- When do these rights revert back to the author?

Rights reversion clauses are important to understand. When and how do the rights revert to the author for this publishing project? Is it based on time, status of the book (i.e., "in print"), or status of sales within a specified period of time?

Remember, a contract isn't an "all or none" thing. It's a negotiation.

* * *

Joanna: Just a quick word from me in this chapter as I have chosen not to pursue traditional publishing in English language for my books (at this point in my career).

Part of this has to do with being a relaxed author, because every time I consider submission and the process of working with agents and traditional publishers, I make the active choice to continue with the indie route because of the freedom and control I have this way.

I have signed foreign rights deals and will certainly consider other licensing options, but for now, I am a happy (and relaxed) indie author!

Resources:

- *The 7 P's of Publishing Success*
  — Mark Leslie Lefebvre

- *Publishing Pitfalls for Authors*
  — Mark Leslie Lefebvre

- *Closing the Deal… On Your Terms: Agents, Contracts, and Other Considerations*
  — Kristine Kathryn Rusch

- Stark Reflections on Writing and Publishing Podcast. Episode 145. Robert J. Sawyer on Leveraging Your IP and Hybrid Publishing — www.starkreflections.ca/robertjsawyer

2.3 Value your work. You create intellectual property assets. Retain control as much as possible.

Joanna: When you write a book, you create an intellectual property asset. You make money by licensing your work in different ways — by format, by territory, by language and by term (amount of time).

Publishers are not charities. They want to license your intellectual property in order to make money with it, so make sure you understand copyright and the many ways you can license your work.

You might think that a relaxed author just leaves contracts and details about intellectual property to someone else.

But you'd be wrong.

If you think that, you might sign this increasingly common contract clause: "World English for all formats existing now and to be invented, for the term of copyright."

If you sign that, the publisher controls your intellectual property asset for 50-70 years after your death and if they choose not to publish an ebook in Australia, or an audiobook in the USA, or if they stop publishing the book altogether, then tough luck. You have signed those rights away.

A relaxed author educates themselves on copyright and rights licensing and understands the value of their work.

They sign contracts for selective rights, for example, German language in Germany, Austria and Switzerland for ebook and paperback, for a ten-year term. Or single narrator audiobook rights in English for seven years.

They might also be happy to sign away all rights for a big enough chunk of cash that enables a relaxed life — but most authors don't get this!

A relaxed author learns about contract clauses and retains as much control as possible so they have a choice for the future as new technologies and opportunities emerge.

For example, J.K. Rowling retained her ebook and audiobook rights to Harry Potter and has since built Pottermore, which made £32.5 million (around US$45 million) revenue in 2020, according to The Bookseller. Many other authors with traditional publishing contracts signed an addendum for digital rights without understanding what that might mean for their future income.

A more current example is the emerging trend for creators to issue limited digital editions as NFTs on a blockchain. If you've signed away "all formats existing now and to be invented," then you can't take advantage of this emerging opportunity — and there will be so many more in the future.

* * *

Mark: Step back and consider your over-arching IP, instead of just the book itself. Particularly when it comes to audio.

With the traditional contract I signed for six of my non-fiction true ghost storybooks, I signed over audiobook rights and the publisher has never produced an audiobook. But fortunately, that wasn't the dead-end for audio.

Think outside the book

I tried to get those terms changed in my contract. The publisher refused. But here's where a revelation came to me that freed my mind, and my anxiety.

When I think of it just as a book, I lock myself into something that's restrictive and stressful. I signed over the audio rights to *Haunted Hamilton* that I am not getting back any time soon. Worrying about this will not help me.

But what is the book *Haunted Hamilton*? It's a bunch of chapters written about different ghosts and locations I researched that were compiled into a book that is available in print and ebook formats and available from the publisher online and in bookstores.

But all the research I did, all the notes I took to write the book are still mine. They're part of my greater IP.

The book *Haunted Hamilton* is merely one incarnation of that greater product.

Understanding that, I have been able to leverage new technologies that draw upon this research.

Such as *Voice Map,* a GPS location-based smartphone app that offers virtual audio walking tours. I compiled some of my research notes about Hamilton, along with new resource and research material, and created a virtual ghost walk tour of downtown

Hamilton in my voice. It's additional passive income that likely also helps me to sell more of my books, because the virtual tour informs listeners that other stories and details appear in my book.

In addition, I continue to get paid speaking engagements, talking about the stories that went into *Haunted Hamilton*.

So, while I don't have the audiobook rights for that book, I have leveraged audio based on the IP that generated that book in multiple other ways to earn revenue.

Even if you believe you've painted yourself into a corner, if you step back and look at the greater IP, as opposed to just the book that resulted from it, you almost free yourself up again. You're able to recognize that there are other assets, other technologies that may allow you to make relaxed decisions.

Resources:

- *The Copyright Handbook: What Every Writer Needs to Know* — Stephen Fishman
- *Rethinking The Writing Business* — Kristine Kathryn Rusch
- *Selective Rights Licensing: Sell Your Book Rights at Home and Abroad* — Orna A. Ross and Helen Sedwick
- *The Magic Bakery: Copyright in the Modern World of Fiction Publishing* — Dean Wesley Smith
- *Closing the Deal … on Your Terms: Agents, Contracts and Other Considerations* — Kristine Kathryn Rusch
- *How to Make a Living with Your Writing: Turn Your Words into Multiple Streams of Income* — Joanna Penn
- *Hollywood vs. the Author* — Edited by Stephen Jay Schwartz
- NFTs for Authors — www.TheCreativePenn.com/nfts

- Empowering authors around copyright. Interview with Rebecca Giblin — TheCreativePenn.com/rebeccagiblin

- The importance of editing and why authors need to understand their publishing contracts with Ruth Ware — www.TheCreativePenn.com/ruthware

- The Society of Authors (UK) — SocietyOfAuthors.org

- The Authors Guild (USA) — AuthorsGuild.org

- The Alliance of Independent Authors (global) — AllianceIndependentAuthors.org

- Pottermore sales and profits rise with 'strong' Harry Potter sales. The Bookseller, Jan 14, 2021 — www.thebookseller.com/news/pottermore-sales-and-profits-rise-strong-harry-potter-sales-1232915

- Stark Reflections on Writing and Publishing Podcast. Episode 105. Location Based Storytelling with Voicemap — www.starkreflections.ca/tag/voicemap/

2.4 Publish at your own pace

Mark: One thing that can cause you needless stress as an author is setting a publishing pace that doesn't match what you're comfortable with.

When you set a pattern of releases, you also set reader expectations. The fans who follow you are going to come to expect that same consistent pace. That's why stockpiling a handful of books for rapid release, then settling into a different pace for an on-going schedule can be stressful for you, as well as for the reader. (We don't want relaxed readers — we want them enthusiastic and excited about our next book — but we don't want our readers upset by changing the expectations along their reader journey)

If you publish at a particular schedule and the readers are used to getting those books at a certain schedule, it's not fair to change that. But it's also not fair for you as a writer to set a rapid release pace if it's not a pace you can maintain. We often say that a writing career is a marathon, not a sprint. It's almost like when you're learning to run and you recognize the importance of being able to hold a conversation at the pace you are running. If you can, you can usually maintain that pace for a lot longer.

Getting winded by an overly aggressive publishing schedule is going to cause you additional stress and anxiety. Think about yourself as much as you think about the reader, not what you expect to give to them. Give yourself and the reader the benefit of that for a long-term author career marathon you can enjoy together.

***

Joanna: Newcomers to the indie author community seem to think that rapid release is the only way to be a successful independent author, but that is just one way to publish and it doesn't suit everyone.

It certainly doesn't suit me.

Rapid release involves writing several books in a series and then releasing them quickly, for example, one a month, every month, in order to stay high in the Amazon charts, as well as running launch campaigns for those books.

While this might be a successful approach for some, it only suits authors who can continue to produce at this pace. To be clear, this is no comment on 'quality,' which should really only be judged by the reader. There are many authors who write fast, sell tons of books to happy readers and make lots of money. Nora Roberts is one example in traditional publishing, and Lindsay Buroker is a successful indie fantasy author with the same approach.

As much as I sometimes wish I had that kind of brain — I just don't!

If you try to write at a pace that isn't natural and fun for you, it's very like that you will burn out and hate the process. If you try to publish at the rapid release pace and can't sustain it, then you will also end up with unhappy readers.

I've never rapid-released anything.

I finish a book, go through the editing process, publish it, then move onto the next project. I usually put up a pre-order when I have a finished draft ready for editing and I allow a good buffer of time to account for life happening. I have other things going on other than writing, so I don't want to publish at a pace that jeopardizes that.

Resources:

- *Publishing Pitfalls for Authors* — Mark Leslie Lefebvre

2.5 Publish wide (or don't)

Joanna: I started self-publishing back in 2008 when ebooks were still mostly downloadable PDFs and people listened to audiobooks on tape. Self-publishing was still a matter of printing a load of books and selling them by hand at events, which I did in Brisbane, Australia, where I lived at the time.

When the international Kindle launched in January 2010, I had one on pre-order and once I started reading on it, I knew it would change the market for readers — and for authors. I could reach the world with my words and that was truly exciting!

At the time, only US authors could publish direct on the Kindle, so I used Smashwords to reach readers. That was the beginning and since then, the market has exploded globally with many more sites to buy and sell digital ebooks and audio, as well as print-on-demand options.

I'm an English author but I consider myself multicultural. My close family has members from England, Nigeria, Canada, New Zealand, Fiji, South Africa, and the Caribbean. We have Jews, Muslims, conservative Christians and atheists in our family.

We are truly mixed-race — and that shapes my outlook on life.

I want my books to be available in every country, on any device, in every format and able to be bought in any currency, and to be available for free in libraries.

These principles drive my decision to publish wide with my English-language books under my two main brands — Joanna Penn and J.F. Penn. I've now sold English-language books in 163 countries with (hopefully) more on the way.

Being wide is relaxing for me because I publish everywhere and market online and I know readers can find my books wherever they choose. As I retain my rights to all formats, I can take advantage of whatever new opportunities arise.

I rarely look at my sales rank on Amazon because it doesn't matter. I often sell more books direct from my website than I do on the big stores on launch, which means I keep more of the revenue. I measure "bank, not rank," a well-known saying within the Wide for the Win Facebook group.

Being wide with my main author brands also suits my pace of writing and publishing. I don't feel the pressure to rapid release or chase the algorithms in KU. I am more relaxed knowing that I have diversity through multiple streams of income, and I particularly love selling direct from my own site, which is not possible if you're exclusive.

All that said, **I absolutely understand that some people find it more relaxing to be in Kindle Unlimited because it means they only have to focus on one platform**.

I have some books in KU because of my limited ability to market them wide. My German non-fiction books under Joanna Penn and my mum's sweet romance as Penny Appleton are all in KU so I can take advantage of free days and auto Amazon Ads, which work for those books. I have no other way of marketing them and they are 'set and forget' books, so KU is the most relaxing and easiest option for me.

Note that these are not 'rapid release' and KU is certainly not just for those people writing a book a month. So, I understand that in some cases, going exclusive will be more relaxing.

Only you can make the choice for your situation — and of course, you can change your decision over time.

* * *

Mark: Authors need to do what works best for them and allows them to be more relaxed. If being exclusive to a single retailer is easier and causes less anxiety, then great.

But for me, publishing wide is about recognizing our ultimate lack of control. There are so many things about the world, and about the book industry, that we can't control. I sometimes think that having a wide mindset is a way to optimize your chances on the roulette wheel that is the publishing industry.

An exclusive mindset means having one chip that you put on a single space on the roulette wheel.

A wide mindset means having a dozen or two dozen chips that you can spread across 20 different spaces of that roulette wheel.

Yes, the payoff's potentially going to be different, and it may take many more spins of the wheel to achieve the same jackpot totals, but you're less stressed about having it all rest on a single fateful spin.

For anyone who assumes I might be immediately badmouthing or talking smack about Amazon (perhaps justifiably, because they're the only major player who forces writers to make the exclusivity decision), let me share one example from one of the other major five retailers.

In October 2013, Kobo, one of the most author-friendly retail players in existence, shut down every single indie-published title in their catalog without warning.

It was part of a major snafu related to their UK partner WHSmith, for whom Kobo is the ebook provider. A news outlet found a few titles within the erotic category that went well beyond spicy/hot erotica. These titles involved incest, bestiality, and other fetish content that, by comparison, would make *Fifty Shades of Gray* look like sweet or inspirational romance.

I was at the helm of Kobo Writing Life at the time, and the offending titles had come in through that portal and distributors like Smashwords and Draft2Digital. At the time, there were no proper filters in place to detect such content, and, with no ability to distinguish illegal pornography from erotica, Kobo executives had no choice but to shut all self-published titles down.

My team and the entire Content team spent endless

hours for weeks working hard at manually vetting all those delisted titles to bring them back online as quickly as possible. But the damage had been done. It's a real-life example of a time when authors woke up to find their books delisted from an entire global catalog without any warning. These titles were here today, gone tomorrow.

The rules can change at any time for whatever reason that has nothing to do with you and how hard you've worked.

And to know that a company like Kobo that cares so much about authors can do that, anyone can do that, anything can happen at any time.

You don't need that kind of stress hanging over your head if your entire author career depends on a single retailer.

Resources:

- *Wide for the Win: Strategies to Sell Globally Via Multiple Platforms and for Your Own Path to Success* — Mark Leslie Lefebvre

- *Release Strategies: Plan Your Self-Publishing Schedule for Maximum Benefit* — Craig Martelle and Michael Anderle

- Facebook group Wide For The Win — www.Facebook.com/groups/wideforthewin

- Facebook group 20 Books to 50K — www.Facebook.com/groups/20booksto50k

2.6 Sell direct to your audience

Joanna: If you own and control your intellectual property rights, you can sell direct to your audience in multiple formats, as well as distributing your books through all the established vendors.

I've been selling my ebooks direct from my site for over a decade through various means but in the last two years, the sales have increased substantially as readers have become more used to it, especially with more people shopping at various sites online during the pandemic.

I also find it more relaxing to know that I can reach readers and sell books without relying on the major platforms.

I don't intend to pull my books off those sites, but they could change the rules at any time, and inevitably, companies rise and fall as time passes. As we write this book, there are Bills in the US Congress to regulate or even break up Big Tech and new laws being debated in the EU about limiting the power of the companies that we rely on as indie authors.

We don't know the ramifications of these changes

or how long they will take to shift the existing eco-system, but this is my career and my income, so I intend to protect it for the long term, and that means building income streams I control.

Benefits of selling direct

You receive a higher royalty on selling direct, usually 80-90%, even after factoring in platform costs and bank fees. You also receive income in your bank or PayPal account within hours of payment, sometimes within minutes, compared to months or even years through publishing in other ways.

Some readers want to support authors and independent creators and understand that buying direct helps financially.

You can also reach readers across the world who might not have access to purchase on the other platforms, or those who don't want to transact on certain sites for ethical reasons.

When selling on existing platforms, you never know who buys your book. If you sell direct, you know who the reader is, although of course, you need to comply with anti-spam and data protection regulations like GDPR. You can integrate the platforms with your email service and market to readers directly without relying on the distributors.

You can also market to existing readers without having to rely on advertising, which eats into profits on the vendor platforms. As long as you have an email list, you can reach readers with an offer.

Selling direct is a great way to make income quickly by offering value to your audience. In the early days of the pandemic in 2020, anxiety was high, the stock market crashed, and we were all worried about making money in increasingly tough times. I emailed my list with a discounted offer to buy direct and made several thousand dollars within 24 hours, money in my bank account immediately that really helped in those first difficult months when everything felt out of control.

How to sell ebooks and audiobooks direct

There are different digital solutions for selling ebooks and audiobooks online, but make sure you investigate how they handle digital taxes. The EU has specific (painful) digital tax rules and increasingly other jurisdictions are adding them too.

I use Payhip to sell my ebooks and audiobooks, which integrates with Bookfunnel for delivery, as well as integrating with Stripe and PayPal for payment. Payhip manages EU digital taxes, enables promotional coupons and other marketing options. Bookfunnel delivers the ebook to the reader's preferred device and to the Bookfunnel app for audio. They also manage customer service and help readers to access the book if they have trouble.

> For more detail, check out my tutorial at TheCreativePenn.com/selldirecttutorial

I also use AuthorsDirect through Findaway Voices for audio, although this is only available in specific territories at the time of writing.

Other options include WooCommerce, SELZ, Gumroad, Shopify, eJunkie, and Fastspring. Remember to check the tax options as you investigate further.

Sell print books direct

Many authors sell print books at conferences, conventions, workshops, readings, speaking events, or even local markets. You can purchase your books in bulk from your publisher or buy from Ingram Spark or other printers, then sell for a profit.

You can also sell print books directly to readers

from your website or sites like Etsy or eBay, but most authors only do this for a small volume of signed copies for super fans or as a marketing activity. You have to manage stock, storage, and shipping so it can be expensive and time-consuming.

If you want to sell print directly, you can use something as simple as a PayPal button on your website. You can also use Payhip and some other digital options for physical products, or more extensive solutions with options for drop shipping through Shopify or other providers.

If you publish print books through Ingram Spark, you can also use Aer.io to create an online store for your print-on-demand books, or use Bookshop.org for a curated bookshelf of your books. Both of these services are territory-specific.

Should you sell direct?

Even though you can make higher royalties selling direct, there are monthly fees for each of the services, so you need to make a certain amount per month to cover those costs.

If you're a new author with just a couple of books and no email list, it won't be worth it until you've grown your backlist and your audience.

If you care about ranking on the online stores, then selling direct is not for you, either. No one sees your direct sales and they don't count toward any bestseller lists.

If you're more established with a number of books that you have the rights to distribute and an email list to reach people with your promotions, and you care more about money in your bank account than ranking, then selling direct might be worth doing. Only you can assess the potential for your situation.

How can you sell more books through direct channels?

I mainly sell books direct by telling my audience about it, as I am doing here in my books and on my podcast. Link to buy direct from your book pages, and offer discounts for readers to buy direct on your email list and through your books.

> If you want to try the process as a customer, you can download *Successful Self-Publishing* for free in ebook and audiobook format at:
>
> Payhip.com/thecreativepenn

If you're interested in what might become part of selling direct in the future, check out my podcast discussion on NFTs for Authors:

TheCreativePenn.com/nfts

* * *

Mark: While I haven't seen nearly the same volume as Joanna in this area, I do sell ebooks and audiobooks direct via my website and tools such as Authors Direct from Findaway Voices.

A decent portion of my print book sales come from in-person sales via conferences, conventions, comic-cons and craft fairs where I typically invest in travel and purchase a booth/table. For those events I usually acquire my print books via a local printer (shipments from Ingram in the US to Canada can result in exorbitant shipping costs that significantly reduce my margin), as well as discounted author copies purchased from some of my traditional publishers.

One benefit of those in-person events (though, admittedly, I haven't participated in any since 2019) is the connection that you can have with readers, both those who are already familiar with your work who come over to chat with you, and new readers who are enthusiastic to learn about you and your work first-hand and get a personally signed copy. While the cost/investment of money and time in these events can result in reduced margin, sometimes the long-term benefits of those fans who feel a more intimate connection with you result in a far greater word-of-mouth marketing impact.

Resources:

- Payhip for selling ebooks and audiobooks direct
  — www.TheCreativePenn.com/payhip

- Buy ebooks and audiobooks directly from Joanna — www.Payhip.com/thecreativepenn

- Process of using a Payhip coupon — www.TheCreativePenn.com/payhip-coupon

- Bookfunnel for delivery of ebooks and audiobooks
  — www.TheCreativePenn.com/bookfunnel

- Joanna's tutorial on selling ebooks and audiobooks direct with Payhip and Bookfunnel — www.TheCreativePenn.com/selldirecttutorial

- The Ultimate Guide to Selling Books on your Author Website by the Alliance of Independent Authors — SelfPublishingAdvice.org/selling-books-on-your-author-website

- NFTs for Authors
  — www.TheCreativePenn.com/nfts

2.7 Don't let piracy and plagiarism derail you

Joanna: Many new authors worry about plagiarism and piracy, and sometimes, fear of it stops them publishing. Established authors can also spend too much time, money and energy on these issues. But can we really be relaxed about piracy and plagiarism?

Let's start with definitions.

Piracy is the unauthorized use or reproduction of someone's work without the proper license and permissions. Pirate sites have unauthorized versions of ebooks, music and other digital products which people can download without paying.

Plagiarism is taking someone else's ideas and creative work and passing it off as your own. A notable example in the romance community was #copypastecris in 2019 when a Brazilian author committed "multi-plagiarism on a rare and scandalous level," which included plagiarizing Nora Roberts and 40 other authors to create romance books.

My personal approach is to be aware of these things, but not worry too much.

Most readers are wonderful and want to support creators and will buy on their preferred site and in their preferred format, especially if you have developed a strong author brand where you foster relationships with readers over time. You don't need to worry so much about piracy if your books are available in all the usual places, including libraries, and in every format. Also, many pirate sites are phishing sites rather than book distributors so don't click on links to your books if you go looking!

In terms of plagiarism, most authors are wonderful and if they are inspired by your work, they will credit you in their books and acknowledge quotes and you will benefit from cross-promotion. I always include a Bibliography in my non-fiction and I have an Author's Note with my influences and a book list in the back of every one of my novels.

If you want to take it further, there are some practical tips in the resources section, but for me, a relaxed approach is about focusing on writing and fostering reader relationships first.

* * *

Mark: I look at piracy as not losing a sale but gaining a reader. I probably would not have sold the product to whoever pirated my book because that's not what they do, it's not who they are. And I'm not going to be able to change how people behave. But I can relish the idea of perhaps having gained a reader. And I look at that as a potential win.

In a 2020 Immersive Media & Books Consumer Survey Dr. Rachel Noorda and Dr. Kathi Inman Berens found that book piracy can often lead to book sales, either directly or indirectly. Below is an excerpt from page 39 of their 79-page February 2021 report.

> "Surprisingly, pirates avidly buy books. They do not simply steal books and dart away. Pirates' book buying and borrowing rose across all media and in all venues (bookstore, online, library) during the pandemic. For example, book pirates are buying books that they discover in libraries: 58.4% of pirates bought a book at the bookstore that they first discovered at a library. 54.3% of pirates bought a book online that they first found in a library (compared to 35.9% of the general survey population)."

I don't worry about pirates. And sometimes I celebrate them.

I remember the first time I saw a book I had published that had not been available anywhere except a handful of bookstores as a unique print-on-demand product. This was the original version of the anthology *Campus Chills* in 2009 that was launched on an Espresso Book Machine in three Canadian bookshops.

When I saw a scanned version of it up on a pirate site, it actually thrilled me that somebody worked so hard to pirate my book. Because, to me, it meant they wanted to read it and share it with such conviction and intensity that they went to a lot of trouble to do that. I responded by making the work broadly available via greater POD distribution and also releasing an ebook version. If people wanted it that bad, why not make it easy for them to acquire via legal methods?

So, for me, gaining a reader is a lifetime long-term thing, losing a sale is a single action today.

And I try not to stress out about those one-off 'loss of sales' as much as I think about the long-term growth of my reading audience.

Plagiarism is different. That's another writer trying to take your work as their own. It can be as frightening as identity theft.

This might be another reason why wide is actually a more relaxing option, because authors whose books are only available on KU have sometimes been plagiarized and put onto the other stores because they're not available there.

So, if you are available in all the stores, you may be less targetable for plagiarism.

I try not to worry much about it, too. If it happens, you deal with it. Spend time focusing on positive things, rather than trying to narrow in on and only look for the negative, which can have a negative impact on your overall sense of being.

I sometimes wonder if this might be a 'whoever fights plagiarism' kind of thing. Nietzsche said, "Whoever fights monsters should see to it that in the process he does not become a monster. And if you gaze long enough into an abyss, the abyss will gaze back into you." I'm not suggesting that worrying about plagiarism is going to make you a plagiarist, but I do worry about the effect of spending time focusing into that darkness.

Actually, I take a page from Joanna's book, of doubling down on your authenticity because that community, that supportive community of other writers and other readers, are probably going to be the people that will discover a work of yours that might be plagiarized.

Other people are looking out for you because they care about who you are and the brand that you've built. And that's part of the benefits of nurturing a community. It's easier to establish that when publishing wide because your people may not all be in a specific single channel. They are all over the place, digitally, and geographically, and you don't know where they're going to be. But they're out there, they know who you are and what you're made of. And when you're authentically part of that larger community, exposing the frauds, the plagiarists, becomes that much easier.

Resources:

- The Indie Author's Guide to Managing Piracy by the Alliance of Independent Authors — www.SelfPublishingAdvice.org/indie-authors-guide-to-managing-piracy
- The Indie Author Guide to Managing

Plagiarism by the Alliance of Independent Authors — www.SelfPublishingAdvice.org/is-copyright-broken-part-2-the-indie-authors-guide-to-managing-plagiarism

- If you want to check your own work in case you have inadvertently plagiarized someone, you can use tools like ProWritingAid — www.TheCreativePenn.com/prowritingaid

- Nora Roberts files 'multi-plagiarism' lawsuit alleging writer copied more than 40 authors. The Guardian, 25 April 2019 — www.theguardian.com/books/2019/apr/25/nora-roberts-files-multi-plagiarism-lawsuit-alleging-writer-copied-more-than-40-authors

- Insights from the Immersive Media & Books 2020 Consumer Survey. Stark Reflections Podcast Episode 147 — www.starkreflections.ca/2021/05/14/episode-191-insights-from-the-immersive-media-books-2020-consumer-survey/

- Immersive Media & Books 2020 Consumer Survey, via Panorama Project — www.panoramaproject.org/immersive-media-reading-2020

2.8 Deal with cancel culture, bad reviews and haters

> "There is only one way to avoid criticism: do nothing, say nothing, be nothing."
>
> *Aristotle*

Joanna: It is a scary thing to put your words into the world, because once you publish, other people can read what you think — and many of them have opinions and thoughts that you might not want to hear.

Writers are often sensitive people, and words are powerful to us. We are far more likely to pay attention to the few nasty reviews or comments than we are to remember the positive ones.

I could say that a relaxed author ignores all this altogether, but I'd be lying! Realistically, you just have to accept that you will probably face some form of these things at some point and you need ways to handle the situation.

Cancel culture is a form of censorship that usually involves social media attacks or even mainstream media drawing attention to someone whose views don't fit with a certain group. It appears on all sides of the political spectrum and takes a polarizing position rather than appreciating nuances of discussion.

Haters are a form of this and usually involve more direct action like emails or bad reviews.

These things are less common than you think but they are over-hyped by the press so it seems like they're everywhere. I've been publishing since 2008 and I have only had a few incidents of nasty emails and comments on social, which I just immediately blocked and deleted.

Bad reviews are far more common, and absolutely to be expected as part of the normal author life. Personally, I don't read them. Some authors will say it's useful data, but not for me. My little brain just melts down into misery, so as long as my star average is over three and a half, I don't worry about the one and two star reviews. You can't avoid them, you can just decide whether to read them or not.

How do you stay relaxed about publishing when these potential things might happen to you?

If you think your work might attract attention from a certain group because of a topic you cover, then it might help to have beta readers or sensitivity readers who can help you think through whether you have addressed all the right issues and avoided things that might trigger others. For example, when I co-wrote *Risen Gods* with J. Thorn, I asked a male Maori reader from my community check that we had written in a way that would not offend people. I had an Indian reader check *Destroyer of Worlds* for the same reason.

If you find that social media comments destroy you, then consider opting out altogether. For example, I stopped doing Facebook Ads because they needed monitoring and some of the negative comments ruined my day. You can, of course, outsource ads if you have the budget, and you can even outsource your email inbox if you really want to filter out the nasty comments.

> **Find a process that will help you stay on the happy and creative side of being a relaxed author.**

* * *

Mark: I think it's no different from writing your first draft with the door closed, with your editorial self firmly locked outside, and letting the creativity, passion, and words flow. And then afterwards, you are respectful of Strunk and White's *The Elements of Style,* and the rules of good grammar, solid dialogue and ultimately polishing your prose. You can also then take a respectful look at characters, situations, and cultures that make up your book. So, in my mind, it's another layer. It's another pass in the writing.

I think it's important to see it as a draft or an edit, rather than a finished product. And definitely not something that would stop you from publishing a book, for example.

Because you can be afraid of who it might offend while you're writing it. In the last novel I wrote, the bad guys are part of a Neo-Nazi, white supremacy hate group. I had to have characters in that novel do and say things that were dramatically against my personal belief system. It offended me just looking up nasty slang words to have my characters call people because I needed it to be authentic.

And that was a challenge. I almost stopped writing it because I was so afraid I was going to offend the people I was defending and standing beside. But I had to keep reminding myself of that extra layer in the process, that analytical part of looking at the text, would come at the next step. That would be where I would step back and consider elements of respect and sensitivity, the same way a developmental editor might help with the plot structure and character development. Or the way a line editor might help tighten your prose.

We shouldn't let fear or anxiety of the editorial process prevent us from writing an authentic first pass.

And, similarly, we shouldn't let those same anxious thoughts concerned about sensitivity and respect, block that first draft.

I think we need to let ourselves go and write the story that resonates, allow those dark or disturbing, or unedited and uncensored words and scenes, and dialogue to flow, at least in that first raw pass.

Then, after we finish, we take the time to craft and polish not only the grammar, but also the sensitivity inherent in the work we have created. That's where we can cut, trim, revise, adjust, and ensure the work does what we've intended, perhaps invoking the desired sentiment, theme, moral, but ensuring it's not actually harming or offending.

When it comes to reading reviews, for good or for bad, I have never shied away from them. I'll even read the one- and two-star reviews.

Maybe it's because I grew up through the traditional side of publishing, where the rejection would come from an editor or agent, rather than a downstream reviewer. Prior to getting my first works published, I'd faced hundreds of rejections.

So maybe all of those things have helped me develop a bit of a thicker skin.

I've actually leveraged negative reviews in a positive way.

Here's how I look at it. Somebody who wrote a review took the time to express their emotional reaction to what you've written. That's powerful; whether their reaction was positive or negative.

So, the part of my writing spirit that is constantly striving to be better looks at reviews as something that can help improve my writing.

A negative review is going to teach me one of two things. The first one might be that my book got into the hands of the wrong person, which is most likely the case. They're not my target audience. So maybe my marketing or positioning of the book was off in a way that made them believe they were going to get one thing, but ended up getting another.

Is there something I can do to fix that or not? A different cover, a different blurb, changing my targeting and marketing efforts to align more with reader expectations?

I did that once, when, after reading a critical review, I realized a subtitle I'd used for a mini story collection was misleading. It was *Snowman Shivers: Scary Snowmen Tales*

The review mentioned that the stories were more funny than scary. I was setting up the wrong reader expectations. So I changed both the cover (the original was a bleak snowy landscape; the updated one featured a dark humor photo of a snowman swallowing a kid, legs and boots still sticking out of its mouth) and the subtitle. It became *Snowman Shivers: Dark Humor Snowman Tales*.

Those changes have helped readers know, better, what they can expect. And I feel that reading that review constructively and applying the update, makes me more relaxed. I now feel more confident that fewer readers will feel misled as to what they can expect in that themed chapbook collection.

Understanding what you can change and what you can't is also important.

Because it might not be the marketing, or the positioning, or whatever. It might just be a miserable person who hates everything. If that's the case, I'm never going to make them happy. And part of it is trying to recognize that, moving on and accepting it for what it is.

In other cases, where it's obviously the intended audience, but there was something that didn't work for them, I like to recognize that they took the time to say something that did not work for them.

Most people don't leave reviews. But if someone actually put that much conscious thought and effort into leaving a review to express what didn't work for them, understanding what that is might help me.

I leveraged plenty of editorial rejections with critiques in them to help improve my stories before sending them to other editors and markets when I was traditionally publishing. So I try to do the same thing with a review that contains potentially useful details.

There may be something a reader points out that helps me recognize an element I missed in my writing. I may not go back and update that specific work, but I might apply it to my future writing. It might help me develop and learn and grow as a person and as a writer.

But it's definitely not easy. Because many reviews don't come with useful critiques. And it is easy to become consumed in the negative.

I would strongly advise that writers do not read their reviews, especially if they haven't developed a thick skin.

Perhaps the relaxed author makes a choice that's best for them. They decide whether to read any reviews at all, whether to read only four and five-star reviews, or whether to even look at the one and two-star reviews.

A few potential strategies for using reviews:

Because reviews *can* derail authors, here are a few options to consider:

Don't look at reviews at all, just look at the overall star rating. This allows you to get a feel for the average reaction from readers.

Only look at positive reviews. Although be aware that some four- and five-star reviews can still contain critical things that might put you off your game or cause you stress and anxiety.

Have a virtual assistant or trusted friend go through your reviews to pull out things that you could:

- Use in review quotes or blurbs to help you really understand what resonated with a reader, or what they loved. (Useful for revising blurbs, or other marketing related activities)

- Pull out into bullet points or even re-worded to help inform or instruct you as you continue to better yourself in the craft of writing.

The relaxed author just makes good choices. Personal choices. Understanding what they are comfortable with and rolling with it.

Resources:

- *The Successful Author Mindset: A Handbook for Surviving the Writer's Journey*
  — Joanna Penn

- *Resilience: Facing Down Rejection and Criticism on the Road to Success*
  — Mark McGuinness

2.9 Find a community who support your publishing choices

Joanna: When I starting self-publishing in 2008, I was living in Brisbane, Australia. None of my friends were writers and when I went along to an in-person writing group, they were horrified when I talked about self-publishing.

So I went onto Twitter, which was a new social network back then, and found authors who understood my situation. I started a podcast to meet other authors and these days, many of my friends in real life are people I met on social media and then asked onto my show, and later met up with for coffee or gin. In fact, Mark and I met online well before we ever met in person.

When I moved back to the UK in 2011, I went to a literary festival and once again, I felt judged for my publishing choices. But once Orna Ross founded the Alliance of Independent Authors in 2012, I discovered an in-person and online community I was proud and happy to be part of.

While it is valuable to have a community of people

in your area, you might find your most supportive author friends online. Use your feelings as a guide when deciding how appropriate a group is, because it might take some time to find the right fit.

If you write zombie horror or paranormal romance, don't join a literary fiction group.

If you are adamant that being an indie author is the best choice for you, don't join an MFA writing group that focuses on finding an agent and traditional publisher.

If you want to write one book every year and publish wide, don't join a group that advocates rapid release into Kindle Unlimited.

If you want to write a book a month and focus on KU, don't join a group that focuses on slow but steady growth on multiple platforms over the long term.

Find a group who accept and support your choices, where you feel a positive energy that inspires and encourages you during the inevitable difficult times.

* * *

Mark: The reason Erin Wright came up with the idea of the Wide for the Win Facebook group was a need to bring together like-minded indie-authors within a community.

Within the author community, the divide between Amazon exclusive (or KU) and Wide was almost as big as the 'indie versus traditional' publishing gap.

If you wanted to learn how to indie publish, the loudest voices, and the biggest platforms seemed to be all about Amazon all the time. And not a lot of beginners will have the ability to take the information shared within those massive silos and then digest it with a much-needed grain of salt to apply a non-Amazon-centric viewpoint.

The thing about Wide for the Win that is valuable is the community by default isn't Amazon-centric; it's open and accepting of different paths available for authors to climb, and so you can find discussions about finding success on many other major retailers and lesser-known digital sales platforms.

Community comes back to the idea that you often become most like the people you spend the majority of your time with.

Wide for the Win is very vague. 'Wide' is a generic

term. 'Win' is also. How do *you* define a win? It's pretty open to how you want to do things. Some other groups out there are very prescriptive and narrow in their approach or even just by the titles they have adopted.

Names are important.

Consider ALLi, the Alliance of Independent Authors.

ALLi suggests that we're allies, we're friends, we're going to support you. The other day I was telling a writer about why it was so valuable to join ALLi. Even sharing their name 'Alliance of Independent Authors' speaks to what it is. You immediately get that feel of a community that is supportive. And ALLi's definition of 'independent' does include traditionally published authors with an independent mindset. That's inclusive. That's definitely WIDE.

* * *

"Spending time with other authors in a similar place to me is an instant mood lift. No one gets writing like other writers get writing. I belong to one writing group where people show up at the same table in a library every Tuesday morning, and we write. We pause to chat and say hi when people arrive, ask questions and sympathize when things go wrong, but mostly we just work near each other. This creates an amazing synergy that really kicks the feelings of isolation to the curb."

Gillian St. Kevern

Resources:

- Alliance of Independent Authors — www.allianceindependentauthors.org
- *Networking for Authors* — Dan Parsons
- Interview on Networking for Authors with Dan Parsons — www.TheCreativePenn.com/networking
- Facebook group Wide for the Win — www.facebook.com/groups/wideforthewin
- Facebook group 20BooksTo50K — www.facebook.com/groups/20Booksto50k

Part 3: Relaxed Marketing

3.1 Focus on the basics first

There are so many ways to market a book that authors can easily become overwhelmed by the options, trying everything at once and struggling to gain traction.

> **A relaxed author focuses on the basics first — and also understands that you need to do the best you can at publication, but you can always change things later.**

First of all, your book should be the best you can make it, because there is no point in marketing otherwise.

Then the basics of marketing include understanding your audience, and deciding on your book title, sales description, book cover, genre or categories, and keywords.

We will not go into the technical details as we both cover that in the various books and tools linked in the Resources section. These chapters are more about what we have learned about being a relaxed author around marketing.

***

Mark: If you are providing the best content that you can at the time as opposed to a half-baked version, you'll be more confident in marketing it because you'll be proud to show it off. Because if it's not the best you can do, there may be a subconscious limiting or sabotage of the marketing at play.

It might be like when you don't finish the book, falling back on the thought of: "If I never put it out there, I'll never get judged." But in this case, it's more along the lines of, "I didn't work to market it because it's not the best I can do."

Be careful that you're not giving yourself these pre-excuses. It's one trap you can fall into.

Ultimately, though, when I think about the basics for being relaxed, I want to go right back to the beginning before you're even thinking about where you're going to spend your money.

And it's thinking about the audience.

Because you can be the most relaxed when you're thinking about who is going to enjoy this story. Often we write books with someone specifically in mind or some intended or imagined audience. And that audience may even be us.

For example, Joanna writes thrillers because she enjoyed Dan Brown and studied theology and religious history. She applied that in a book she wants to share because she enjoys that type of thing as a reader. She knows who she is writing for because she is among that demographic.

But **thinking too much about yourself instead of the reader can lead you down the wrong path**. It's an error that I have made.

When I released *A Canadian Werewolf in New York*, I did not consider it to be urban fantasy, despite the fact my main character is a man who turns into a wolf and has enhanced senses and abilities when in human form. I don't actually read much urban fantasy. And I didn't think it would appeal to urban fantasy readers because in my novel you never really see the wolf, you only see the man. So, I originally went with a cover that did not match the urban fantasy novel look and feel. That original cover took a more literary style and the subtitle was "A humorous thriller."

It was my readers who informed me where I'd gone wrong.

Reflecting back on it, I'm positive that most literary readers wouldn't actually enjoy it. I completely missed focusing on who the ideal reader was. It's a fun action thriller in a world that has sprinkles of the paranormal. It's likely not going to appeal to someone who reads novels of high literary merit. They're not my readers. My readers would more likely be fans of Jim Butcher or Kelly Armstrong.

When I had the covers redone in 2020 both for that book and the rest of the on-going series, that simple rebranding of those covers for the proper audience worked effectively.

The original version of the cover came out in 2016. The revised version came in 2020. Interestingly, four years on, I sold far more copies of the novel than I had when it was first released.

I'm glad I didn't panic when I came to realize that four years earlier, I'd made a huge mistake. I think **what's important is the understanding that it's not set in stone**. You can change things, like the cover, the blurb, the branding. I changed the cover. And I also changed the blurb several times over the years.

The first time I modified the book synopsis, I hired Bryan Cohen, founder of Best Page Forward, to help me. I used that for several years. But in 2020, when I was revising the cover, I also re-revised the blurb to incorporate something an early reader and one reviewer had said, as well as inspiration from a conversation Joanna had with a guest on an episode of The Creative Penn podcast. It was a fresh, new, and more fitting logline.

The changes weren't all at the same time. The blurb changed, and then changed again, and then the cover changed, and then the blurb changed again. That is the brilliance of being an indie author. You're not locked into having to wait on or convince your publisher to make a change, then wait for the current print run to run out so they might consider investing the time in making those updates, which they aren't likely to do anyway.

Those updates, those changes you can make as an indie author are part of the on-going process of learning and growing. The more you learn, over time, about who is reading and resonating with your work, the more you can adjust and tweak and incorporate the things that are most likely to draw others like them in to your work.

* * *

Joanna: One benefit of being an indie author is how easy it is to change things over time because you are in control of your book. Of course, you want to do the best you can when you first publish, but inevitably, you will discover aspects you want to change.

It's also natural to rebrand over time as your career progresses. Many traditional publishers rebrand covers and re-release bestselling and classic books. It's a normal part of publishing, so you can be relaxed about making changes later. I have even changed a number of book titles because I learned more about my audience.

Book titles are a critical element of marketing. Non-fiction readers are searching for an answer to a problem or more information on a specific topic, so the title, or at least the subtitle, must make that clear.

Fiction readers are attracted to the emotional promise of specific genres, so your title must resonate with that. I have been wrong about both of these!

My first non-fiction book was originally called *How to Enjoy Your Job or Find a New One*, self-published in 2008. I didn't sell very many copies even when I discovered how to publish on Kindle. But then I discovered the importance of keywords and found the keyword phrase 'career change,' which people searched for all the time.

I re-edited and re-titled that book to *Career Change* in 2012 and it continues to sell because people search for the topic. Changing just the title of the book increased my sales without doing any more marketing, although of course, I also changed the cover to match.

Since then, I have titled my non-fiction books in a way that makes it obvious to the reader what's inside. You can even research keywords before you settle on a title.

Fiction titles are more complex. We all understand the power of words, and your title needs to resonate with your target market.

My first three ARKANE thrillers were originally called *Pentecost*, *Prophecy*, and *Exodus*. I am not a Christian but I have a Masters in Theology and all my fiction delves into questions of faith and the supernatural as well as being set in places rich with religious history.

In some of my early reviews, readers noted that they thought they were getting Christian fiction because of the titles, but the books are actually thrillers in the vein of Dan Brown's *The Da Vinci Code*. So I changed the titles to *Stone of Fire*, *Crypt of Bone*, and *Ark of Blood*, rebranding the covers to make it clear they are action-adventure/conspiracy thrillers.

Over the last decade, I have also changed book covers as well as categories and keywords, and updated my sales descriptions. That is just part of being an indie author. So do the best you can when you publish, but **relax and understand that you can change things later if you want to.** There's nothing wrong with that. It doesn't mean you failed. It just means you've discovered more about yourself as a writer and your book — and that's an important part of the author journey.

Resources:

- *Successful Self-Publishing: How to Self-Publish and Market Your Book* — Joanna Penn
- *Wide for the Win: Strategies to Sell Globally Via Multiple Platforms and for Your Own Path to Success* — Mark Leslie Lefebvre
- *How to Market a Book* — Joanna Penn
- *How to Market a Book: Over Perform in a Crowded Market* — Ricardo Fayet
- Publisher Rocket. Tool for Categories and Keywords: www.TheCreativePenn.com/rocket
- K-Lytics. Research for specific Amazon categories: www.TheCreativePenn.com/genre
- List of book cover designers and a tutorial on how to find and work with cover designers: www.TheCreativePenn.com/bookcoverdesign

3.2 Simplify your author brand and website

Joanna: When you have one book under one author name, you can easily keep things simple! But over time, if you get the bug for writing, you may end up with lots of books and sometimes, several pen-names.

The advice is mixed on whether to use multiple author names. Some say it's better to separate genres by different pen-names in order to clearly define your readership and make it easier for the algorithms to serve your books to the right audience.

Others say that publishing everything under one name is easiest to maintain and if you use different cover branding for different genres, readers will be able to find the books they want to read.

> **A relaxed author makes a choice on whether to use more than one author brand — and maintain more than one website.**

I started out with non-fiction under Joanna Penn and published my first two novels under the same name. But in 2014, I decided to split out my fiction under J.F. Penn. I built a new website and set up a new email list and it was definitely the right choice for me.

It helps me focus my time as I allocate it by author name, and my book cover branding is clearly differentiated. I'm also a different persona as J.F. Penn — more introspective and much quieter! I enjoy separating my readership and some of my fiction audience don't even know I write books for authors.

It's also a good idea to consider what you want to do with your website. Will it just be a list of your books, a few pages of information, and an email sign-up? Or do you want to have regular content like a blog, podcast or videos on a topic around your book?

I started TheCreativePenn.com as a blog and a podcast, and JoannaPenn.com forwards to a landing page within it.

I started JFPenn.com as a static site to list my books and email sign-up and BooksAndTravel.page as a second podcast a few years back, which also links through to my books and email list.

I also have CurlUpPress.com, which is a static site for my publishing imprint. It lists my books and has an email for potential licensing partners.

You definitely don't need as many websites as I have!

But for me, the relaxed option is to split out my author brand and sites, rather than have them all in one place. Only you can decide what's best for you — and of course, you can always change your mind later!

* * *

Mark: I had been building my author brand, Mark Leslie, since '92 when my first short story was published in a magazine. I dropped 'Lefebvre' when submitting and publishing my fiction because it's a name people have difficulty spelling and pronouncing. Mark Leslie was a far easier name for most people. I suppose I had been thinking about 'marketing' in 1986 when I'd started submitting my writing to publishers when I considered the average person's ability to remember how to spell or say a name when looking me up or someone might try to recommend my work to a fellow reader.

But in parallel, I had built a name for myself within the bookselling and indie author community as Mark Lefebvre. When *The 7 P's of Publishing Success*, the first of a half-dozen books I wrote for writers was released in 2018, it was important for me to leverage my existing name recognition or the 'brand' that some authors knew me as.

Otherwise, I would have considered keeping everything under Mark Leslie for simplicity's sake. But there is the additional factor of a clear split depending on what people are looking for.

- *Mark Leslie* writes horror, Twilight Zone style fiction, true ghost stories, thrillers, and urban fantasy.
- *Mark Leslie Lefebvre* creates content to help authors understand the business of writing and publishing.

Similar to the way Joanna has split her pseudonyms, there's a clear divide.

But I link everything related to me back to *www.markleslie.ca*, which was the initial brand I use, and is far easier for people to spell, type out, and find.

Because of that merger to a single website, I realized a number of people signed up for my author newsletter, not because they cared about my fiction at all or even knew about it or wanted to know about it; they signed up because I was a voice in the industry, and they wanted to hear what I had to say.

So what I've had to do over the last year, is slowly trying to move people out of that Mark Leslie Author Newsletter and into a non-fiction business of writing and publishing newsletter where they're actually going to get what they're looking for: information and insights based on my experience and things I'm paying attention to in the industry.

I had inadvertently attracted many of the wrong people to my author newsletter, and that led to poor conversion rates that messed with my stats. It made every email look like a failure because if the content was not associated with non-fiction writing and publishing stuff, those readers didn't care. They don't care about my werewolf stories or my ghost stories. For my author newsletter, I want rabid readers, I want the ones who are hanging on for the next release under that 'Mark Leslie' banner.

So I tried to parcel things off, and remind those who sign up for 'Mark Leslie' that this is not where the business of writing and publishing happens. Nope; that comes from my Stark Reflections on Writing and Publishing Newsletter.

Similar to the learning I shared in the previous chapter, about having the wrong cover that didn't match the genre or reader expectations, I realized things weren't set in stone. I could change them. So I did.

I also took the time to not be frustrated that my fiction/ghost pseudonym newsletter was, and still is, filled with other authors, curious about what I'm sharing as an author. Because I've established a brand as a trusted book industry representative and voice, I have to accept that, and not let it upset me. I attend to what other authors are doing all the time. It's one way I continue to learn. So how can I be upset when there are other authors wanting to do the same thing? We are, after all, in this together. So I have come to accept that my Mark Leslie Author Newsletter is likely never going to hit those optimum conversion rates. But it doesn't mean that the actual readers on that list aren't being delivered what *they* are looking for.

Owning the platform is important

When you own the platform, rather than depending upon another party, you reduce the stress and worry about what might happen if it changes or goes away. Twitter, Facebook, Instagram, TikTok, whatever platform you're working at for community-building, can shift, disappear, completely alter. But your own website, with a domain that you own, that's solid and lasting. And you're in control of it.

But you don't have to break the bank to establish your own presence. And it doesn't need to be elaborate and packed with frills.

When you first start off, try to keep it simple. Don't spend $10,000 or whatever in creating some custom-designed website. Use standard themes for WordPress or standard plugins so that you are future-proofed.

You can choose an inexpensive host at the beginning because you won't have that much traffic. But ideally, paying at least a moderate amount to own the domain reduces stress and worry. If you have a simple website built on a platform that has terrible terms and conditions and it's free, *you* are the product, and they can take it down, and they can advertise on it, and all of the above.

This goes for podcasting as well. There are so many platforms that are free, but you have to consider who is the product and what is the monetization method? If you want to be relaxed in the future, you have to give yourself the control.

A relaxed author is in control of their intellectual property and their assets. And these marketing assets include your website and your email list.

3.3 Simplify and automate your email

A relaxed author has an email list because it means you can reach readers without having to advertise and you can sell books regardless of what happens to the platforms we currently rely on.

There are some initial hurdles to overcome in order to set up your email list, and it might be stressful initially, but it's definitely more relaxed over the long term.

Mark: My email is very much like passive income. I used to work hard to get people on my lists, and I stressed out about it. But then I got more stressed out because most of the people I worked at getting onto on my list were not on the list because they cared about what I was writing; they cared about a free book from *anyone.*

And so I gave up on that rush to the top of trying to get 10,000 people or 100,000 people or whatever, and I would rather have 10 dedicated readers than 100 or 1000 wishy-washy people who don't care about who I am or what I'm writing.

So, that was a difficult learning process for me. But a good one. And one that has helped me become less stressed.

Grow your audience slowly with quality readers

Yes, I want people to sign up for my list, but I want them to sign up for my list for the right reasons. And it is important to build a list, but I would rather it be built organically based on the readers' desire to have to want to know what the next thing is that I'm doing. They sign up because they don't want to miss out on my next thing, not because I backed them into a corner and forced them onto it.

Come to think of it, perhaps your newsletter helps your readers themselves be less stressed because it's an assurance they won't miss that next book release.

While I want to grow my newsletter, I never want to be stressed out about how many people signed up this week, or how many people unsubscribed after getting their free ebook.

Life got a lot better when I stopped thinking of the newsletter as an advertising broadcast to my audience and started embracing (following Tammi Labrecque's advice) my newsletters as if they were an email to my best friend, sharing some tidbits about what's going on in my life. That's fun. That's enjoyable. That's relaxing.

That approach has also helped weed out the people who don't care about my life in a really effective way. For me, thinking of the newsletter as passive marketing has dramatically helped me.

A lot of authors get stressed about, "What do I email people if I don't have a book a week?"

I like to share what's going on in my life. I am a pretty open person online. I'm quite the open book. I share a lot of things, maybe too much (particularly if you ask my partner, Liz). But I'm comfortable and fine with that.

Because part of my passion is craft beer and dad jokes and skeletons and parody videos, my newsletter incorporates those elements.

I have a very small auto-sequence to make sure that they've got the free ebook and they're opening the emails. But after that, they may not know who I am. So the on-going monthly newsletters provide that.

And I always want to give them more. I want them to have additional access to deals and notifications and insights before anyone else. But I'll also always remind them how they can get my books for free because I want to give them stuff. If they care about my writing and I give them things they'll likely appreciate, we are curating a solid virtual relationship. I think that's a great way to behave in general. That's that 80/20 rule. Give 80% of the time, ask 20%.

Of course, interacting with your readers can sometimes be a mixed blessing. Because if it's that popular, you could spend a lot of time engaging, rather than writing new books.

However, I feel that time spent engaging with a reader is a way more valuable long-term marketing strategy than a good number of the various marketing strategies authors are told to invest in. Connecting with someone who really resonates with your writing is creating a moment; it's creating something that is probably far more powerful than running a single ad you spend a lot of money on and you're hoping to get a return on. The kind of return you want is that powerful engagement. So, one way of looking at it is that the time you've invested in that relationship may actually be more valuable to you long-term than some scheme of whatever the current hot and popular trend you're hearing about that 'all authors have to do.'

* * *

Joanna: I have a 'set and forget' mentality around growing an email list which helps me remain a relaxed author. I have used the same Reader Magnet, my Author Blueprint, on The Creative Penn since 2008, although I update the material every few months to keep it current.

My sign-up at TheCreativePenn.com/blueprint has been the same since then as well, so every time I put it in a book or mention it on a podcast, the call to action remains evergreen. It is a 90-page PDF on everything to do with being an indie author, from craft to publishing and marketing and I haven't published it anywhere else.

In terms of staying in touch with readers, I email every two weeks to my Creative Penn list with links to content, any promotions or launches, and an update on my writing, with personal pictures as a glimpse into my life.

For my fiction, I have a free ebook at JFPenn.com/free and again, I have used that same link for many years so even if people have an old copy of one of my books, they will be re-directed to whatever my latest Reader Magnet is. I use the Pretty Links plugin on WordPress for my redirects but you can find options for whatever site you use.

I email my readers every few months with pictures from my Instagram @jfpennauthor and notes on my book research trips, as well as deals on my fiction, new book releases, and recommended reading within my genre.

I use and recommend ConvertKit and I have set up automations (also known as autoresponders) for both brands. These are a series of automatic emails that introduce people to my various books and pages of content, and for J.F. Penn, it includes an invitation to join my Pennfriends Street Team (also known as an Advance Reader Review List) once someone has been on my list for six months.

When I started out, I definitely had a more formal tone in my email, but I try to keep more of a chatty, personal vibe now. You don't have to use the same language in your email as you do in your books. In fact, it's a good idea not to! You want to develop a relationship with your readers over time, so they know your name and care about your books.

If you want more responses to your emails, then ask questions. For example, in my Creative Penn email,

I might ask, "How's your writing going this week?" For J.F. Penn, I'll ask, "What are you reading?"

This has the benefit of building a two-way relationship with people over time, but in terms of being a relaxed author, I recommend setting aside time to answer emails once you have a bigger list as you can get a lot of replies — and that is a mixed blessing!

Resources:

- Tutorial on how to set up your email list with ConvertKit — www.TheCreativePenn.com/setup-email-list
- *Newsletter Ninja: How to Become an Author Mailing List Expert* — Tammi Labrecque

3.4 Find one form of marketing that you enjoy and can sustain for the long term

Joanna: There are many options for marketing and of course, you're welcome to try as many of them as you have tolerance for — but you do not have time in your life to do everything!

You have to choose what to focus on and **a relaxed author decides on one major form of marketing** for the long term that also fits with their personality and lifestyle choices.

You have permission to stop doing marketing tasks you hate!

If you try to do everything, you will be stressed and overwhelmed. If you try to sustain marketing tasks you hate, you may give up the author life entirely because you will lose the joy that brought you to writing in the first place.

If you want a long-term author career, you have to write and you have to market, so why not choose something you enjoy and can sustain?

I've tried pretty much every kind of book marketing since I started publishing in 2008 and it is important to give things a try as you don't know what might resonate. After years of experimentation, I settled on podcasting and audio as my main marketing channel. I love attraction marketing and find it the most relaxing. I put something into the world and you find it somehow and choose whether to engage.

No push push.

No hype.

No interruption.

Just a slow attraction and word of mouth over time.

I started The Creative Penn podcast in March 2009 and I've created consistently since then. It's now an income stream with paid advertising and Patreon support and I love talking to other authors about aspects of the writer's journey. It's useful to my audience and I also enjoy it for my own development.

I started my Books and Travel Podcast in 2019 as a way to explore the places behind my fiction and my love for travel and the show is a mix of personal reflection and interviews with other authors. It is a passion project right now, but it feeds my creative soul and tangentially brings people to my fiction.

Plus, I have a travel memoir on the way, so it will be more direct marketing at some point.

In terms of other content marketing, I no longer write blog posts, although I create show notes with a transcript for my podcast episodes. I don't do written interviews (unless it's for major media), although I will happily go on other people's podcasts and radio shows for an interview. I occasionally do video, but I don't focus on it.

I have other marketing activities as covered in separate chapters but my primary focus is podcasting, which is creatively fulfilling, financially rewarding and great for book marketing. It works for me, but of course, you will have to find your own preferred method.

* * *

Mark: I think what's really important in the example Joanna shared is that she tried a bunch of things, but then did biofeedback and looked at what she felt most comfortable with. When you do that, you understand what you're willing to give up, and what you're not willing to give up. That can really help when you're getting started and trying to figure out all the different types of marketing and social media available for content marketing.

But the thing that you focus on can change over time.

And you don't have to prevent yourself from making a change by telling yourself, "Oh, I made this decision. I have to stick with it."

If it's not working, if it's not making you happy, then stop doing it. Because if you're enjoying it, if it's something you wake up and look forward to engaging in, that's a good thing. It's an important aspect because at the very least, the participation and involvement in that task gives you pleasure and you're going to have a much more relaxed approach to your day.

Embrace authentic diversity

The other thing for me is that I thought I was ruining my brand by being too many different aspects. I'm:

- Mark Leslie Lefebvre, the book industry guy
- Mark Leslie, the horror author
- Mark Leslie, the true ghost story writer
- Mark Leslie, the urban fantasy author

But I'm also Mark the dad joke guy, the Spider-Man fan, the craft beer lover, the guy who makes silly parody videos, the man with the skulls and the skeletons.

For a long time I stressed out, thinking I was doing myself a disfavor by not focusing in on one of those elements and just going with it.

But the truth is, I'm not happy only being one thing.

We may be one thing to one person, and something else to another. But even in our most intimate and meaningful relationships, we're often way more than just one thing to that person.

And I realized that I'm perfectly fine with being all of those things. I enjoy the complexity of it. So, I was needlessly stressing out thinking it was causing me to not be as effective when it came to marketing and selling myself and my books and my brand. And I realized that **is** part of my brand, and so embracing the authenticity allowed me to accept that strange complexity.

What I have found is that the right people who appreciate that complexity, or even just one or two aspects of the greater whole, seem to gravitate toward it naturally. So embracing that fully authentic multidimensional person I am has improved my interactions and engagement. It hasn't stifled that at all.

One of the biggest challenges I see facing authors is when something is trending, whether it's social media or a specific marketing tactic, and they believe that *this new thing* whatever it happens to be, is the magic bullet for marketing success.

At the time that we're writing this book, everyone is thinking, "Oh, TikTok is how you're going to sell books and find readers." Or: "I need to be on Clubhouse and gather a huge following there." Similarly, they get a powerful FOMO because they're not doing Facebook Ads, or Amazon Advertising, and they hear that's all the rage.

This never changes. New social media, new platforms, new marketing tools and tactics will always arise. There will be waves and trends.

And people will flock to it and get excited on how it can help them launch their brand, their books, their sales, into the stratosphere.

Yes, there is always potential. And luck. And some strange algorithmic factor that can allow any of that to happen.

But most often, and for most people, it's never the magic bullet they were looking for.

It may have seemed to have been the magic bullet

for the first handful of people who were there to ride those first few gigantic waves up, but usually, the mass group that comes along behind might not see the same sort of lift.

And that makes for automatic disappointment. And stress.

Because those who come along after seeing Johnny and Janey Success stories are ultimately scrambling to purchase lottery tickets at the corner store where some lucky bloke won the big jackpot the week before.

I often equate this to a bunch of ten-year-olds playing soccer.

There's that first lucky kid who has the ball and is running down the soccer field, happy as a clam and excited as all-get-out. But the rest of those 10-year-olds are just running madly after that one kid with the ball. None of them are happy. They're all stressed out.

And when another kid gets the ball and rushes off in a different direction, the entire pack shifts and follows that kid.

The one with the ball is ecstatic.

Everyone else is clamoring to be that one kid.

Instead of playing their own positions. Strategically. Patiently.

We often fall pretty to wasting a lot of time and energy stressing out about the next big platform as opposed to looking at it from a more personal, "Is this something I enjoy?" point of view.

Or, to partially return to the soccer analogy: Is this my position, my role? And, does this fit in with my skill set, my comfort level, my passion on what I enjoy spending my time doing?

Trends, whether they are social media, marketing tools or strategies, change and morph. The book industry itself continues to see significant trends and shifts, ebbs and flows of what is selling when and where and why.

Understanding and paying attention to those trends is important. But wildly chasing them back and forth across the field is only going to make you more stressed out.

* * *

# These authors found ways to relax around marketing

"Figuring out what works for my marketing style as opposed to what others think is best has helped me relax. As an author, I want to connect with people, so as a publisher, my marketing needs to reflect that. Focusing on the joy of storytelling helps a lot. Realizing this career is a long game also helps. Having multiple streams of income takes the pressure off the novels and lets the stories find their audience in their own time. A series I first published four years ago is finding a wider audience now, because the time is right."

T. Thorn Coyle

"I let go of the early notions drummed into my head that our books have to make a huge Amazon splash out of the gate and then the shelf life of the book is incredibly short. Once I figured out that is complete rubbish, I could breathe again."

Kimberly Diede

"Another thing that has stressed me out during these last few years is the insistence that the ONLY way to succeed (or reach the top level) as an indie author is to pour a lot of money, time and energy into ads.

I've done all the courses, learned the ropes, made moderately successful ads ... and I've hated every minute of it. It was only about 8 months ago that I gave myself permission to stop fussing with ads and instead find my own way to success. In my case, that meant growing my income by expanding my income streams, with a focus on the fiction app/serialization space. I haven't reached my financial goals yet, but I make a comfortable living and I'm SO MUCH more relaxed and even excited about the 'business' side of my business (for the first time in a long time!)."

Ember Casey

"I want to be known for my writing, not for my marketing. I'm fine seeing less profit. Life is too short and too unpredictable to take hours away from my family in order to game Amazon."

Anonymous

Resources:

- *Audio for Authors: Audiobooks, Podcasting, and Voice Technologies* — Joanna Penn
- The Creative Penn Podcast — www.TheCreativePenn.com/podcast
- Books and Travel Podcast — www.BooksAndTravel.page/listen
- Stark Reflections on Writing and Publishing — www.StarkReflections.ca

3.5 Put book 1 in a series free or permafree and schedule regular promotions

Joanna: I love having permafree first in series ebooks because I can schedule regular promotions on them. New readers discover my writing every time and may buy more of my books.

I don't have to remember to change my prices and I can add links to the free books in my automated email sequence as well as mentioning them on interviews and on social media without worrying whether the promotion will still be valid.

It's easy to do if you publish wide.

Set the ebook to free on Kobo, Apple and Nook and then report the lower price to Amazon who will (eventually) price match. Check out my thriller *Stone of Fire* or *Successful Self-Publishing* on any ebook platform to see it working in practice.

If you're exclusive to KU, then you can't do permafree but you can schedule five free days every 90 day KU period. My mum's sweet romance as Penny

Appleton is in KU and I log in every 90 days, schedule five days free for each book at different times of the month and then book a Freebooksy for *Love, Second Time Around*, the first in the series.

There are many options for price promotions but my relaxed options are:

- Use **Freebooksy** to schedule a promotion on the free book. They will also remind you by email when it's been a while since you last advertised, which is handy!

- Use the **Kobo Promotions tab** to apply for free promotions as often as possible. You won't get them all but they definitely sell books at Kobo. *Note:* You have to publish direct to Kobo Writing Life for this option and request access to the promotions tab.

- Use **BookBub Pay Per Click Ads** as a campaign. Of course, applying for a BookBub Featured Deal is a great idea, but they are difficult to get, whereas you can always use the BookBub ads to reach readers. I recommend *BookBub Ads Expert* by David Gaughran on this topic.

* * *

Mark: I don't yet have a first full-length novel in a series free. That's partially because, until just recently, I never followed my own advice to start writing in a series, despite having recommended that to authors for years. I'm still playing catch-up in that regard. So, I will eventually very likely have book one in my Canadian Werewolf series free.

Currently, I have a 10,000-word prequel short story published that is free everywhere in ebook format. The audiobook is for sale at a low price, but I also have a free version of it posted to YouTube. And the call to action at the end informs readers that this is the original 10,000-word story that inspired the novel *A Canadian Werewolf in New York*, the first full-length novel in that series.

When you sign up for my newsletter, I offer a free short story collection. I don't have enough books in any one series to be able to offer the next book for free for newsletter sign-up. I've changed what that free book is over time and will likely continue to evolve this strategy as I produce more work.

In addition, I have several stand-alone free short stories and mini story collections so that new readers can sample my work, get a taste for my fiction, and then potentially move on to other story collections, or even my novels.

You don't need a series to leverage that 'First Book for Free' strategy

I also have a good friend, Sean Costello, who has written nothing other than stand-alone thriller and horror novels. He has a permafree stand-alone, and then offers a second stand-alone novel for free when people sign up to his newsletter. That can work as well. Because typically, once a reader falls in love with a writer's work, they'll come back for more of the same, even if it's not part of a series.

It has worked for Sean, both for newsletter sign-ups, and for read-through of his other stand-alone novels. Sean's longest running perma-free title has just under 7,500 reviews with a 4.2-star average rating on Amazon. And the average total of reviews/ratings of his eight other stand-alone novels comes to about 350. His author newsletter engagement continues to be solid despite him not having released a new book since January 2017.

Resources:

- *BookBub Ads Expert: A Marketing Guide to Author Discovery* — David Gaughran
- Freebooksy is just one of the paid promotional newsletter options at WrittenWordMedia.com

3.6 Choose social media that suits you — or don't use it at all

Mark: The thing we forget about with social media is we get so hung up on "How am I going to leverage this to sell something?" and we forget why it exists.

It exists to connect people.

It's just another way of people connecting with one another.

And so I try to think about social media as walking into a room and seeing people having a conversation and then either butting into that conversation with something that's completely off topic, and not appropriate to the stream of what's happening, or becoming a part of that community. It should be a community that you want to be a part of, a conversation you naturally want to be involved in. You're not trying to change the conversation, but you're trying to be a part of it and offer something to it that benefits everyone.

That approach, to me, is a lot more real. You come in and listen in and watch what's going on. And if you don't like this conversation, you don't find it engaging, you move on to a different platform where you can find and engage with your people.

If you go to a writer conference and there are groups of writers who work in certain genres and they're all engaged in specific topics pertinent to that genre, you rarely try to fit your desired discussion points from your genre into the wrong group. You move to find the group speaking about the same elements, topics, discussion points.

Whenever you see comments from writers who feel at home in a particular social media setting, or themed writer group community online, they often express the idea of finally feeling at home and comfortable. They use phrases like: "I'm so glad I found my people."

If you don't have that feeling, it might not be for you.

Think of social media in that same way.

It's a community of people where you're going to meet and connect with a group of other writers, or your potential readers, your ideal readers, your ideal market or audience but in communities like that, by being a part of that, by engaging in that community.

So, when I **think of social media as community as opposed to marketing**, my approach to social media is a lot less stressed out, it's a lot more relaxed, it's a lot more of a "This may lead to sales, but I'm not doing it for sales." And that has really helped me in my approach.

Lately I've been playing around and trying to do more audio/video content on YouTube, Instagram, and TikTok because I'm enjoying the fun challenge of what I see as storytelling in a different medium. I've embraced more visual storytelling and I'm learning and experimenting.

It's funny to realize that I'm currently experimenting with stuff that I was engaged in when I was a kid with performing skits onto an audio cassette, with making VHS movies in my teens and then in university when I was involved in theater. I'm applying all those skills and passions in a different format now that I'm a better writer.

But one of the interesting things about that is the same idea, the same IP (Intellectual Property) can be leveraged in multiple formats.

We often talk about evergreen content. But green also means sustainable, renewable resources.

You can reduce, reuse, recycle, in your creative life, too, as a writer, as a storyteller. And you can leverage that to get the maximum benefit of that IP because you haven't wasted it on a fleeting moment as opposed to some non-renewable resources.

Clubhouse is a non-renewable resource; at least in its current state. Because if you're not there at the right time in the right time zone, you miss it.

But the one benefit I think Clubhouse provides is, since early 2020 when the world started to shut down in terms of in-person gatherings, I missed those organic hallway conversations that we would have at conferences.

Often, we would go to conferences just to connect with other writers. And it was more about that for many writers than even the content being presented. Yes, the content drew me there, but half the time I didn't go to many of the sessions. It was those connections I relished.

So one interesting thing about Clubhouse is, in a pandemic world, it allowed for those connections to happen. In addition, it was a great outlet for people who don't like video. It provided a leveling-off of the 'video class system' of those with elaborate backgrounds, or green screen settings, or a higher-resolution camera and professional lighting.

Video can introduce a resounding level of stress. Particularly for those who don't like or are not comfortable being in front of a camera and may even have their camera turned off. But even then, they might be overwhelmed with the quiet judgment they perceive is happening. It can create an unspoken class system.

And let's not forget the virtual video fatigue that we've seen many people express since as early as mid-2020.

Audio platforms like Clubhouse almost democratize that because if you have things to say that are on target with what the discussion is, you're of value and you don't have to worry about not having a good camera, a fancy laptop, or even a weaker Wi-Fi signal.

So, even if a platform isn't evergreen, and is fleeting, it can still be, just like those in-person events, where solid connections happen, a great place to learn, connect, and engage as part of your on-going relaxed author journey.

* * *

Joanna: Some authors use social media effectively to sell books, connect with readers and other authors — and they enjoy the experience. But I think that number is probably small!

Most of us choose one or two networks to focus on and use them as little as possible in order to achieve specific goals.

I joined Twitter in 2009 and it helped me find other indie authors around the world. It truly was my social network when I had no author friends and self-publishing was still considered 'vanity,' rather than a viable way to reach readers and make a good living.

I still use Twitter @thecreativepenn but social media has become a tiny part of my author life and an even smaller part of my business.

If you're going to use social media, then consider the following:

The popular sites rise and fall, so don't build your entire author platform on any particular one

Remember MySpace? Or how Facebook bought Instagram because it was taking market share? Or how TikTok suddenly became the go-to platform?

Sites change the rules

Remember how you used to be able to reach everyone on your Facebook Page or in your Group, but then it became 'pay to play' and you needed to Boost posts? By all means, join social networks that resonate with you, but drive people back to your own website and email list, so you are not dependent on them to survive.

Choose the site/s that suit you and don't force yourself into things that stress you out

I've never really enjoyed Facebook, so I have automated message responses that ask people to come to my website so I don't have to monitor the inbox. I auto-post most content and occasionally do ads but I don't have the app on my phone and I don't log in every day.

I thought I might like Clubhouse for social audio but it is only for live conversations. I prefer evergreen content that I can use to reach people globally, so I ditched that after the first day.

I still use Twitter to find news and post my podcast episodes as well as respond to comments. I use

Instagram @jfpennauthor to post pictures from my travels which I then use in my email newsletters.

I have thought about giving up social media entirely, but it still plays a part in my author life, albeit a small one. It's not necessary to use and I would give it up in favor of my email list and my podcast in terms of book marketing.

Make a choice about how you spend your time and how social media fits with your goals.

* * *

If you find social media stresses you out too much, maybe you should just quit like these three authors?

> "Nothing has helped me become more relaxed than quitting social media two-and-a-half years ago."
>
> *Zach Bohannon*

"FORGET social media. It does not sell enough books for enough authors to be worth the poison. We drive traffic to social media, then social media soaks us for ads and reach. Let's just not, okay?

Readers want the books, they pay for the books. Focus on the books. Focus on your website, and please have one — not a FB page. Focus on your newsletter and on the platform areas that are all about books.

Focus on what you can control, and stay away from the highly manipulative, toxic, cesspit of greed and negativity that is — BY DESIGN — social media."

Anonymous

"Recently I've opted out of a lot of Facebook groups. So much of the information and discussion stressed me out and probably wasn't relevant. Sure, maybe 1% of stuff might've helped increase my bottom line and I'm going to miss out on that now. But I feel the time and peace of mind I've gained more than makes up for it."

Kat Cotton

3.7 Advertise in campaigns, not constantly

Joanna: If you love advertising and it doesn't stress you out at all, then feel free to ignore this chapter. But many authors find it to be one of the least enjoyable aspects of book marketing — and that's certainly true for me.

I remain a relaxed author about advertising because

(a) I outsource Amazon ads as covered in the next chapter, and

(b) I focus on campaigns rather than a constant onslaught of daily monitoring

A campaign has a specific goal and runs for a limited amount of time

This might be the launch of a new book where you have activities spread over a few days or weeks, depending on your goals, or it might be a promotion of a backlist title that needs boosting, for example, a discounted first in series.

Organize the things you want to do with a specific time frame, schedule as much in advance as possible, for example, price changes and ads on various platforms. Then once the period of promotion is finished, **turn it all off and take a break.**

Yes, you heard me right! Turn those ads off, even if they are working, especially if this is one of your areas of stress.

There will always be a tradeoff, but if I have to check ads every day, it occupies 'mind space' that I would rather use for something else. Some days I need to be offline and go for a long walk. Some days I need to focus on creation — my author head — without being distracted by marketing and business. Some days I just need space for my mental health.

Only you can decide how long your campaigns will be, but I am certainly more relaxed when everything is turned off and I don't have to worry. This is particularly true for Facebook Ads, because of the potential for negative comments, so I am pretty militant about only running these occasionally and for a limited time. My mental health and long-term creativity are too important.

Of course, I have evergreen marketing that runs all the time — primarily my automated email (chapter 3.3), podcast episodes (chapter 3.4), and perma-free first in series (chapter 3.5). These things run without me and I don't have to log in and check data or comments, or worry about ad spend. I can just remain a relaxed author … until the next time I run a campaign!

* * *

Mark: One campaign approach, which I borrowed from author Erin Wright, is instead of the stacking that we often do with marketing, consciously spacing them out.

Stacking is when you schedule a series of back-to-back promos with BookBub, BargainBooksy, eReader News Today, Fussy Librarian, and an author newsletter blast, for example, to get five consecutive days of a larger 'trending mound' instead of a 'spike' effect.

When you promo stack, you avoid the single-day spike that might tell the retailer algorithms your book was a one-off flash-in-the-pan, instead of a more consistent hot seller over a number of days. And then, every month, or every 45 days, or based on some consistent cycle, you repeat those stacked promos and keep giving the same book, or alternating books, a visibility and sales and ranking boost.

Spacing is looking at those same half-dozen promo sites/newsletters and cycling through each of them on a weekly basis so that over 30 to 45 days, you can cycle through them, running continual campaigns.

This would be, for example, running a campaign for one promo newsletter on week one, then another on week two, and so on, throughout the cycle.

It means you're not getting a larger mound effect in a single week, but rather a series of spikes, more like a consistent drumbeat over time, at a bit of a more leisurely pace. That constant pattern alerts the algorithms that your book is relevant in the long run.

Finding the pattern of marketing that works for your own comfort level, and then pre-scheduling and knowing the pattern you're going to roll with, can be comforting, like the way a mother's heartbeat is pacifying to a baby.

3.8 Outsource when you can

Joanna: If the author life was just sitting at a desk with a gorgeous view creating new words on the page, we'd probably all be more relaxed!

But it's not.

There are always more things to do in terms of developing your craft, editing, publishing and marketing tasks, email and other aspects of business. The To Do list will never be finished and there is always more you need to action — which is why outsourcing can help you become a more relaxed author.

But be warned, you cannot hire a clone of you. If you try to find someone to do all the things you hate, you will swiftly discover that no such person exists. If you advertise for "someone to do my book marketing," you will end up disappointed and likely declare that outsourcing doesn't work.

I know because that happened to me early on!

The best approach is to write down the specific things that you do and break them down into discrete tasks.

Decide what is most important, then find different people to do each separate thing

For example, I am the only employee at The Creative Penn Limited, but I have freelancers who do various roles:

- Fiction editor
- Fiction proofreader
- Non-fiction proofreader
- Cover designer
- Print book formatter
- Amazon Advertising management
- Podcast transcript editing
- Inbox manager for unsolicited emails through my Contact form
- New Patron management
- Bookkeeper
- Accountant

These are all 'virtual assistants,' in that none of them work full time in my business and I haven't met most of them in person.

I have also hired other people to do more specific tasks like 'create a fantasy map of New Zealand' for *Risen Gods*, or 'Three months Facebook advertising for my ARKANE thrillers,' or 'Improve my website speed.'

While those are tasks in my author life, I also use outsourcing in my personal life. I have a cleaner and I have groceries delivered, both of which free up more time.

Make each task as specific as possible and then look for someone to fulfil just that one thing.

Many authors ask me when they should outsource, and some will say they can't afford it. But trust me, you will know when your stress levels get consistently too high and you feel like you're about to explode with everything you want to do. You will reach a point when you need to eliminate tasks entirely or find someone else to handle them for you in order to become a more relaxed author — and by then, you will be willing to pay for it.

* * *

Mark: I was initially thinking that I'm not as good at outsourcing as I should be. That it's an area of development I need to work on.

But part of what Joanna and I have been discussing about the relaxed author mindset reminds me that part of that is the stress of comparisonitis.

Do I even need to outsource? Or is it just something I feel I need to do because all the cool kids are doing it and I'm experiencing FOMO?

Let me walk through this.

I've experimented with some outsourced admin work. I know I haven't yet found the right match. So that's part of it. It's like a relationship or friendship. You try them out, some are a good fit. Some others don't last beyond the first meeting.

Sometimes, when I have attempted to offload some work and it hasn't resulted in a positive outcome, it's probably just the result of a mismatch. My misunderstanding of the person's abilities or knowledge in an area might have been the issue. Or their perception of working with me didn't align with the reality of the experience. It's not that they weren't good. It wasn't that I'm a useless downloader. It was a compatibility miss.

But the initial training and getting-to-know-one-another process is something that does takes time, often multiple attempts with different people, which can cause frustration and create anxiety.

And that anxiety can be a two-way street.

Think about the person I'm hiring to assist me, and the stress I can cause them because I'm a serial procrastinator. I work to deadline. And having to download a task like transcriptions, for example, would only work if I've scheduled at least a week in advance so that I could give the person I was working with time to get it done.

So part of not-offloading most of my tasks comes from knowing and understanding myself and how I work best.

There is a way I prefer to work that rarely aligns with downloading or offloading tasks to another person. And if I try to change how I work, it's going to cause me more stress, and take far more time out of my day, which will cause further heaps of anxiety. So, most times, outsourcing doesn't reduce my stress, it increases it.

Writers can sometimes cause themselves additional frustration if they spend too much time trying to fit their own efficient processes into a mold that doesn't suit them.

For example, my email inbox was a cause of stress for a long time, because it was ridiculously out of hand. I'm talking tens of thousands of unread messages. Most of them were junk, or informational bits that I didn't need.

Over the years I kept trying to get to *inbox zero*. But the problem, for me, was that the methods being outlined for that didn't work for me. I tried them, and they caused me more anxiety, and felt like a waste of time.

I continued to experiment with different methodologies until, just earlier this year, I finally found the right way of doing it that worked for me. There was a simplified method that was about 70% useful for me. But 30% of it didn't work. So I adapted that strategy into something that works for me. Instead of taking the advice as an 'all or none,' I modified it in a way that works.

That looming email inbox was one of those small things that was always weighing on my mind; most often not even consciously. Every time I turned on my computer, I knew that there was a big overwhelming thing for me to attend to. Now, there are no more than 50 mails in the inbox at any time. Enough for a single page of scrolling.

I've tried to keep it down to zero, but if I travel or have a full day of meetings, it's going to shoot up to and often past 100. When that happens, I work to get it to zero, or within that 50. But I'm very ruthless now about deciding, "Is this actually something I have to do something with?" and making that decision.

Can you afford to outsource?

Another thing that many writers are likely to struggle with is being able to afford to pay someone to do work when they aren't bringing in a lot of money from their writing.

I understand that there are investments a writer needs to make. And being able to free up one's time to get back to that all-important task of writing is likely one of those investments. Hiring an editor, and a cover designer are typically the core minimum of those expenses. But after already having invested several hundred or several thousand dollars into a book that hasn't yet earned that back, how does a writer decide to invest more in a virtual assistant to handle email, or social media, or some other tasks?

There's no simple answer, and that might be something that changes over time.

It's a personal decision. And it will most likely require some experimentation and some additional investment of time and money.

It might become easier as your cash-flow situation changes. If you're earning a specific amount from your existing books, you can re-invest part of that back into hiring someone to offload tasks that allow you to write and publish more, thus growing your author business.

But sometimes, even if you can afford the dollars, it might be the time investment in finding and training someone that can cause you stress. Or it might be, similar to me, that your process doesn't always match with offloading certain tasks. You might energize yourself, or take comfort or pleasure in specific redundant or routine tasks that help ground you.

The key is to find what works for you, for your situation, for your comfort of time spent, money spent, and a trajectory of your author business that isn't stressing you out needlessly.

Outsource where it fits or makes sense

I haven't outsourced certain author or podcasting tasks. For example, I compose my own show notes and do the audio editing for my podcast. I'm only at a little over 200 episodes of a weekly podcast I started in 2018. But part of my weekly process, and my own personal learning and growing as a writer lies in the process of doing that manual compiling.

There's comfort and re-learning in re-listening to my interviews and editing the content together. Since my podcast is Stark Reflections on Writing and Publishing, I reflect on one or two things that my interview or conversation with my guest made me think about. I can't reflect if I don't go through the detailed listening, part of which is finding that 30 to 45 second teaser to edit into the opening segment of the podcast. It's part of the process. And it works for me.

I can afford to outsource that work. My sponsorship and the patron support allow me that option. But the process works for me. So I'm keeping it. For now. That may change. But I'm not stressing about it.

Since mid-2020, I started outsourcing my publicity. I still accept bookings directly via my website form, or when people contact me, because I will not turn down a solid earning opportunity if somebody wants me to speak somewhere. But I have hired a publicist to handle my press releases and find me appropriate bookings.

I first tested him out after interviewing him for my podcast. And, after a trial period of just a few months, I realized how much time he was saving me. And, after a few mismatched opportunities — which can always happen — Mickey and I know one another better. He knows the publicity I prefer to engage in, and the ones that I feel are a waste of my time. He has also increased my reach to new audiences, and audiences I had never been in front of before. So, the time saving, and the increased publicity and reach, and even the occasional uptick of sales I've seen from that, have been well worth the expenditure.

Resources:

- Reedsy marketplace for freelancers who work specifically with authors — www.TheCreativePenn.com/reedsy

- Upwork marketplace for freelancers — www.Upwork.com

- *Productivity for Authors: Find Time to Write, Organize Your Author Life and Decide What Really Matters* — Joanna Penn

- Getting a Creative Edge with Publicist Mickey Mikkelson. Stark Reflections on Writing and Publishing Episode 163 — www.starkreflections.ca/2020/11/20/episode-163-getting-a-creative-edge-with-mickey-mikkelson/

3.9 Embrace who you are. Double down on being human.

Mark: You can't help having all these aspects of things you're naturally passionate about, interested in, and that resonate with you.

They can all play a part in your marketing.

And one mistake I made that caused me a lot of stress is I'm known as Mark Lefebvre, the book industry guy. In other circles, I'm known as Mark Leslie, the guy who writes true ghost stories, the guy who writes horror and thrillers and Twilight Zone fiction. And then I'm well-known in other communities as Mark, the guy who loves skeletons, which connects nicely to much of what I write. I'm also the Mark who loves craft beer and dad jokes, musical earworms and parodies and all those things.

I was stressed out because when I considered my author branding, I always felt I was too scattered. I was trying to focus on simplifying my brand so as not to confuse people.

For example, whenever people would ask me to be interviewed for radio, an article, a podcast, whatever, I'd need to know which Mark they were asking for so I could make sure to wear the right hat. And yes, it's important to understand what the audience is expecting, but over time being uncertain which Mark they wanted was causing me stress.

I was causing that stress to myself. I was attempting to hide or cover up the other aspects of me for those situations instead of just embracing the fact that I am all of these things.

So, for example, when I'm doing a consult with authors, I don't hide the skulls on the bookshelves behind me because I'm a business professional. I may put on a sports coat, but I may still have a skull t-shirt on underneath it. So, you're seeing the complexity of who I am as an actual person, not just that thing you thought I was. I'm no longer trying to hide from those things. And that's allowing me to relax in my approach.

Here I am. This is me. Love it or leave it.

Now, almost not a single day goes by where people don't share one of a handful of things with me, either directly or tagging me in social media. Cartoons, photos, memes, jokes, videos related to skeletons, dad jokes, craft beer, musical earworms.

I was originally stressed out about this almost overwhelming influx of tags and shares and messages; particularly if it was something I'd already seen repeatedly because half a dozen people shared the same thing with me that same week.

But then I recognized something truly important.

They saw a skeleton joke, or a music parody, or a goofy dad joke, and their **first** thought was me; that I'd appreciate it. And they took the time and care to send it to me.

That's one of the biggest compliments you can give a person. "I saw this, and it made me think of you." That's powerful. That's heart-warming.

So I pause and appreciate the beautiful and heartfelt sentiment that led to that sharing.

Repeatedly telling myself, "No. No. No, that's not part of your brand," was holding me back. I stopped limiting myself when I stopped doing that.

Embracing yourself is almost like a Maslow's hierarchy of needs because you first have to realize you are good enough because you're the best you to write your book and you're the only you who can share it in the way that you share it. And that's authenticity. And that leads in the long term, in the bigger picture, to where **people purchase things from people they know, like, and trust.**

* * *

Joanna: I've been blogging at The Creative Penn since 2008 and podcasting and doing YouTube videos since 2009. If you go back and look at the content I created back then, it is stilted, and professional not personal. I am even wearing a pin-stripe suit in one of my earliest author photos. At the time, I worked as an IT consultant, implementing Accounts Payable at a mining company. I was a corporate professional, and that's how I communicated in my early writing and content marketing. It was all I knew.

Over the years, I discovered the importance of the author 'voice,' something almost indefinable that makes our writing unique, and also spills over into our content marketing through audio and video.

But it took me years to find what that really meant for me and relax into who I am and what I care about.

I didn't think people wanted to hear about what was going on in my world, preferring to be useful without sharing personal details. I was afraid of what people might think of my interest in graveyards, religious relics, and the darker side of history.

Now I share a weekly personal update on my podcast and pictures of my travels on Instagram and in my emails. My fiction is full of my interest in religion and death culture as well as action adventure, archaeology, travel, and all the things I love. These are the things that make me unique and that's the only way to stand out in an increasingly noisy world.

It's also important to double down on being human, especially in an era of increasing automation and artificial intelligence.

You can't beat the machines for speed and efficiency, but you can differentiate yourself by sharing in a more personal way.

I enjoy podcasting because people have always connected through voice. If I share my challenges as well as my achievements — and laugh at myself — then hopefully people might want to spend more time with me through my books.

I have tried things that didn't work for my personality. For example, unlike Mark, I don't like live video, or video at all really. I need time to prepare and gather my thoughts in writing before speaking, which is what I do with my podcast. I write everything out in advance, or at least significant notes, before recording.

I've also tried and failed at advertising on Amazon and Facebook because I find it all too complex. I am not a data person and I generally want to spend my time doing something else.

All I can do is embrace who I am and what I enjoy — and that will be different for everyone.

If you share what you love, you attract people who love those things too.

The more authentic you are, the more you will resonate with the people who love your work. And that makes it more relaxing for everyone.

3.10 Think global, digital, long-term marketing

Joanna: I am a relaxed author about marketing because I think in a global and long-term way. This is partly to do with my personality, upbringing and multicultural family, but also to do with my author career choices so will hopefully be helpful for you, too.

I've never traditionally published so I've never done a huge book launch. I've never 'broken out' as they call it in the publishing industry, so I have never had a truly massive monthly income spike. My career has just grown and expanded slowly over the years.

I've always wanted to reach readers all over the world in every book ecosystem from mobile ebooks to libraries, from digital audio to hardbacks, so I have jumped on every platform as they became available.

Once I discovered blogging in 2008 and podcasting in 2009, I focused on the global market across multiple countries, time zones, and currencies. I favor evergreen internet marketing above all else because it leads to long-tail discovery and word-of-mouth recommendation. I have sold ebooks in 163 countries because my website is available globally, and my podcast has been downloaded in 223 countries. I don't run ads in all those territories, I just have books available and people searching online find my content somehow.

Of course, there is always a place for spike marketing campaigns, as covered in chapter 3.7, but **a relaxed author builds for the long term and doesn't get stressed about short-term setbacks.**

This mindset will help you make choices about how you publish and market your books. It will keep you away from the addictive checking of sales numbers and ranking because your income streams have expanded so much, you cannot possibly check them all.

It will help you put books into the world without obsessing about the launch. Instead, you will look at trends over time and trust that more opportunities will arise and markets will continue to grow. Consider the seeds you plant as slowly emerging, growing, and developing into strong trees.

Relax. It takes time to build an author career.
You just have to be patient.

* * *

Mark: A lot of authors get anxious and spend endless hours refreshing their sales dashboard. The stress of looking at your sales numerous times a day can really cause a lot of needless anxiety. Looking at the trend over time is an easier way of understanding the necessary 'biofeedback' in order to measure and modify your author strategy.

Focusing on trends in the long term is going to show you more distinctive and important patterns than single spikes or weird things that happen, which you mostly don't have any control over. Some of them are marketing efforts and others are completely unknown, but often, they have to do with a long-term brand you're putting out there when you're putting your authentic self into the world.

Passive and long-term marketing

In 2019, I sold a book at a physical event because of a marketing effort I'd made back in 2006. I was on *The Writing Show* podcast in 2006 talking about the writing of the very first draft of my novel *A Canadian Werewolf in New York*. And thirteen years later somebody walked up to my author table, spotted my name on the banner, and the aforementioned book, and said, "Oh, my God, Mark Leslie. I remember you from *The Writing Show* podcast." And they bought a copy.

Can you imagine the stress if I'd been waiting and watching to see what the effect of that marketing effort might be for more than a dozen years? It happened to be a serendipitous moment. Something you can't foresee or plan for. However, you can set the scene for the possibility, without worrying about it.

I did something: I published something, I took part in an interview, I created a blog post, I was on someone's radio show or podcast, or whatever. And it's still out there, and if something good comes from it, great.

* * *

> "Focusing on the long-term and building a business little by little every day makes me a relaxed author. The more I focus on the complete journey, I realize the massive progress I have made from beginning to now. If I focus on that, I have a more positive outlook."
>
> *Dan Kenner*

Part 4: Relaxed Business

4.1 Do you really want to run an author business?

Joanna: This is an important question!

I used to think that everyone could be a 'successful' indie author, and that everyone wanted to run their own creative business. But over the years, I discovered that authors have different reasons to write, different goals and financial aspirations, as well as varying temperaments.

If you have a day job that pays the bills, or another form of income that is not related to your writing, you can write what you love without worrying about the results. Of course, you'll never stop wanting to reach more readers, but at least you won't have to obsess about making a living with your art.

> As Elizabeth Gilbert says in *Big Magic*, "There's no dishonor in having a job. What is dishonorable is scaring away your creativity by demanding that it pay for your entire existence … You can always make your art on the side of your bread-and-butter job."

So if you don't want to run an author business, no worries!

But of course, some of us are incapable of working for others. I love running my own business and started my first one back in 2000 at aged 25. I started and failed at several businesses — scuba diving, travel itineraries, and property investment, while my IT contracting freelance business paid the bills for over a decade. The Creative Penn Limited is successful now because I failed so many times and learned valuable lessons along the way. I kept going until I found a business model that worked for my lifestyle and also intersected with the rise of technology that enabled it to work.

Only you can decide what's right for you at the different stages of your author career and in the arc of your life.

If you want to run an author business, then you can learn the skills, many of which I cover in *Business for Authors*.

Here are some questions for you to consider:

- Do you love your current job? Or do you want your art to be your job?

- Do you like to be in charge of everything? Do you have control freak tendencies (in a good way!)? Do you enjoy being independent?

- Do you enjoy organizing lots of different tasks and working together with freelancers to achieve a professional finished product? Or are you excited to learn how to do this?

- Do you love learning about new processes, tools, and technologies, and then taking action on what you discover?

- Can you manage the uncertainty of varying income every month? Do you know how to manage cash flow and set aside money for tax, investments, and difficult times? Or are you ready to learn these financial skills?

A relaxed author actively chooses the path that works best for their book/s, their personality and lifestyle, as well as their stage of life. It certainly doesn't have to be the same choice as mine.

* * *

Being an entrepreneur should mean that you are in control.

Mark: One of the biggest stressors that authors face is that their writer income often depends on the world's biggest bookstore. And, within that, they effectively depend on the unpredictable algorithms that can change at any time, resulting in a complete lack of control.

Having multiple streams of income as a writer allows you to focus less on the worry that you're going to lose out when those algorithms inevitably change.

And that has been extremely important to me.

It's always good to have either a baseline (or a number of baselines) of something that you know you can depend on. If something happens and income source X dries up, you still have sources Y, Z and A to rely on.

I spent twenty-five years working on the corporate side of an industry I was passionate about and loved. The book industry. In 2017, I left that corporate world because I didn't want to wholly depend on it. I had reached a point in my writing and related activities where I knew I could make a go of it completely independently. (For the record, I registered my business Stark Publishing in 2004 when I self-published my first book. It has been a long and slow climb for me. My first writing was published in 1992, and that's when I started earning money as a writer. It has been a slow and steady income growth over more than twenty-five years.)

I loved my corporate day job. Particularly since, from about 2011 I was actively engaged in helping thousands of indie authors succeed. But the job I loved was actually preventing me from the creative life I had always wanted. I was investing anywhere between 60 to 80 hours a week in my work, leaving very little time and space for writing.

So I left at the end of 2017.

I had originally thought I could write full time. But I couldn't leave that desire to help other authors entirely behind.

I recognized that the reason I put in ridiculous hours when I was working at Kobo was the intrinsic reward I got from helping other writers. For me, there is an intrinsic value, not just the monetary value, of doing the things that I know can help push the industry forward.

And so, when the opportunity to work with Draft2Digital came up, it provided two things for me.

It provided a part-time baseline income that would remove one of the stressors of the ebbs and flows of the income from writing and consulting. But it also allowed me to do some awesome things. I got to work with brilliant and talented people to build really cool things for authors.

I struggled with the idea of returning to the corporate world, but I reached a wonderful compromise with Draft2Digital where I could be a part-time consultant, offering them 20 hours out of my week, and reserving the other 20 hours for writing.

That removed the anxiety in a massive way.

It allowed me not just the monetary baseline that would help me, but the intrinsic baseline that I knew I needed in order to focus on the things I wanted to focus on. So, I removed stressors in two areas by testing incarnations of how I defined myself and then landing at that decision.

You do not have to be a full-time writer making all your money from book sales. That has never been a requirement.

I'm not sure why the idea of **having** to be a full-time writer has become such a thing in the indie author community. Because in the traditional publishing world, the majority of authors do not make all their money from book sales. You only have a handful of people, mostly household names most people would know, like Nora Roberts, James Patterson, or Stephen King, for example.

But when you look at folks like Patterson, and King, they also have multiple streams of revenue. It's not all just book sales. Sure, they have a lot of books, but they also have other properties. Movies, television programs, masterclasses.

They have multiple streams of income. And many traditionally published authors have a day job. Either out of necessity or, because perhaps they actually enjoy it.

And many indie authors have a day job. Not just for an additional revenue stream, or a baseline, but out of passion, learning, growth. Or maybe, if their writing income streams are large enough, they dedicate time to volunteer work that brings them that underlying sense of completion and satisfaction.

Because we need to pay ourselves not just in monetary ways, but in ways that enrich and enlighten our very being.

* * *

You don't have to run an author business. These authors decided that they are more relaxed with day jobs.

"Working at a day job to generate most of my income helps me be a relaxed author. I put in my 9-5 each day to put food on the table and give me peace of mind. I can write in my free time and not worry about how much money my writing will bring in, or if I would be able to afford the expenses associated with publishing and marketing my books. It gives me the freedom to write whatever I want, whenever I want."

Steve Alvest

"I consider it a hobby that I'd love to turn into a part-time job one day. Removing the goal of full-time author has helped quite a bit. I can always change my goal later!"

Roland Denzel

"The biggest difference for me came when I sat down and made a business goal and a lifestyle goal. As part of that, I decided I only want to be a part-time author. I set time limits each day. I don't work weekends. Having a clear goal in mind has removed so much stress, I can ignore things that don't fit into my plan, and I have weekends free to be with family or to do other activities/hobbies."

Anonymous

Resources:

- *Your Author Business Plan: Take your Author Career to the Next Level* — Joanna Penn
- *Business for Authors: How to be an Author Entrepreneur* — Joanna Penn
- *Big Magic: Creative Living Beyond Fear* — Elizabeth Gilbert

4.2 Create multiple streams of income

Mark: While I have guaranteed part-time work which brings me a monetary base and intrinsic value, I have diversified my income as a writer over the years.

I earn income from traditional publishing, for books as well as short fiction and poetry. From trade publishers and academic publications as well. Within indie publishing, my more than twenty-five titles are available in virtually every major digital retailer, subscription, and library system around the globe. Thousands of sites. In addition to direct sales options and affiliate income.

I write different genres of fiction and non-fiction. Formats include ebook, trade paperback, hardcover, large print, and audiobook. I have embraced storytelling in audio and video format via social media and new apps, including GPS-enabled virtual ghost walk tours.

I earn income from both in-person and virtual speaking engagements with institutions, conferences, libraries, and other venues. I sell print copies (and the occasional digital product) via in-person non-book-specific events, like local fairs, markets, and conventions. I have both sponsorship and patrons for my weekly podcast.

Smart businesses know that creating multiple streams of income is critical

They can't, for example, typically expect to sell their product or service to a single customer. Most rely on numerous customers and regular repeat business. As things change, and some customers leave for whatever reason, there are other customers there to keep that business running. They also need to consider updating, increasing, and/or changing their product offering.

That's all part of recognizing the importance of multiple streams of income.

Let me briefly fall back to my years as a brick-and-mortar bookseller to illustrate something. There are often titles the bookstores carries that we referred to as 'core titles.' These would be perennial classic titles that you could reasonably expect to find in most English-language bookshops in North America. Titles like Stephen Covey's *The 7 Habits of Highly Effective People*, Julia Cameron's *The Artist's Way*,

The Elements of Style by Strunk and White. Also *The Catcher in the Rye* by Salinger, Huxley's *Brave New World*. Titles by household name authors like Austen, Dickens, Bronte, Shakespeare, or more modern names like King, Rowling, Patterson, Atwood, Grisham. The list goes on.

Those core or common titles consistently sell, so are often kept in stock. But bookstore owners and managers are constantly bringing in new and fresh titles; diverse titles, to inspire, inform, and entertain readers with new content. Some things they bring in succeed and result in new revenue. Some of them don't sell at all, or in minimal quantities. But they keep modifying, changing, growing, and adapting.

They don't see the new things that they try and that don't work as a failure. It's just part of the on-going process of managing a successful business. Learn, grow, adapt, and keep trying, through the various cycles and trends of the industry.

In addition, most physical bookstores operate at a loss for half to three-quarters of the year, with the bulk of their income and profit coming in the last quarter of September through December. During those dry periods, they are still providing services to their communities, but not stressing out about the fact they are operating in the red at certain times, because those other times, the profits significantly make up for it all, and it balances out in the long run.

A successful and relaxed long-term author career is, similarly, going to involve experimentation in terms of new products, new projects, different types of writing, potential collaborations and partnerships. It will involve recognizing the highs and lows of the waves that happen in book sales, and among specific title sales trends.

Having multiple products, many sources of income, flowing in at different times, helps with reducing the anxiety and stress that can come with the various sales trends we experience as writers.

When considering multiple incoming streams that can feed us, we should also look beyond monetary measures.

In addition to the importance of multiple streams of income for financial needs, I don't want to miss out on a different kind of source of income: mental, emotional, and social.

Writers, even introverted writers, need input, stimulation, content, context, all of those things that get meshed and mashed into the stories that we weave.

Sometimes having a job, or working in a different space, with different people, brings a much-needed element to our lives. At the end of the day, for example, when I decompress with my partner and talk about how the day went, we each bring different things to that dinnertime conversation. She was out at the school, interacting with her staff and the students, and parents. I was working from home, but had interactions with authors, with my colleagues from Draft2Digital. So when we sit together at the kitchen table sharing our days, we're bringing fresh new elements, streams of insights and experiences, to that day.

Much of those conversations can lead to context and even content for some of the things I write.

But even beyond those, the stimuli we receive from being open to new experiences, from attending to things we read, listen to, and watch, can open our eyes, open our minds, and open our hearts in fascinating new ways that allow us to grow and mature — not just as a writer, but as a person.

* * *

Joanna: If you want to run an author business, it's important to develop multiple streams of income.

Nothing is stable, corporations least of all, and the global pandemic has only made that more clear as established business models disappeared overnight.

The world is uncertain. Plan for change.

Multiple streams of income can protect you because it's unlikely that they will all fail at the same time.

If you're reliant on one income stream — a single publisher, or one self-publishing distributor, or you only have one client, one product, or one book, what risks might you face if the situation changes?

My main income streams for The Creative Penn Limited are:

- Book sales (with multiple books across multiple series and genres as well as multiple formats and vendors)
- Affiliate income (from multiple partners)
- Course sales (from multiple courses)
- Podcast advertising and Patreon sponsorship (from multiple advertisers and patrons)

I could add speaking and consulting back in if I needed to.

I find it more relaxing to have multiple streams of income — both in terms of riding the ups and downs of revenue from different sources, and also in how I spend my time. I'm not the kind of author who can (or wants) to write fiction every day. I enjoy variability in my working week and different creative cycles during the year.

Today as I write this: I wrote several thousand words of my next thriller at a co-working space, the walk there and back is 12,000 steps so I achieved my exercise goal, I wrote several thousand words of this book; I had a business meeting on zoom, and I recorded a podcast interview. I also created a blog post for BooksAndTravel.page and emailed my fiction list. It's been a productive day working on multiple areas of my business.

It's also good to think in terms of your household streams of income, and this is something that has changed for me in the last year.

In 2015, The Creative Penn made enough money that my husband Jonathan could leave his job and join the company. This was fantastic from one angle because we could work together and it gave us more time to travel without having to ask for leave. It was also necessary for various family health reasons.

But during the pandemic in 2020, Jonathan returned to being a statistician in the pharmaceutical industry. He loves his job, and it's much needed at this time in history, so it's great for him. But I am also a much more relaxed author knowing that we, as a household, have another stream of income that is not dependent on me. I am no longer under such pressure and I've been able to cut back on things that stressed me out, like live webinars.

Things inevitably change. We made the right choice back in 2015, and we made the right different choice in 2020. Only you can find the balance that works for you and your lifestyle goals.

* * *

"One of the things that has helped is thinking in terms of having a creative business, as opposed to an author business. I have other creative facets that feed my soul and have the potential to become a stream of income. So, instead of trying to force a book out every four to six months, I'm indulging creative whims and exploring additional opportunities in my creative sphere."

Braylee Parkinson

Resources:

- *How to Make A Living With Your Writing: Turn Your Words Into Multiple Streams of Income* — Joanna Penn

- Winning as a Hybrid Author. Interview with Kevin J. Anderson. Episode 24 of Draft2Digital's Self-Publishing Insiders Podcast — www.draft2digital.com/blog/winning-as-a-hybrid-author-with-kevin-j-anderson-self-publishing-insiders-ep024/

4.3 Eliminate tasks. Say 'no' more.

> "If you're not saying, 'Hell yeah!' about something, say no."
>
> Derek Sivers, *Anything You Want*

Joanna: Many authors are stressed because the To Do list never ends. In fact, most authors add more to the list every day — things to write, ways to market, podcasts to pitch, ads to manage, social media to scan and reply to, content to create, tools to learn, interviews to listen to, and so on.

Here's the truth.

It will never stop.

The writing life is constant. It's not something you can turn off, or at least I can't! You have to find a way to add boundaries so that you manage potential overwhelm, especially as your career progresses.

When you're in the early days of your author career, you will inevitably say yes to everything. You'll write that article or go on that podcast or speak at that event or join that promotional opportunity or take that course because you're building your platform and your network.

> But at some point, you have to start saying no. And if you want to be more relaxed, **you have to say no to yourself, not just to other people.**

Trust me, I've learned this the hard way by taking on too many things and ending up way too stressed!

For example, I spent several years pursuing screenwriting. I read books, went on residential and online courses, and adapted several novels into screenplays. I listened to podcast interviews with screenwriters and interviewed some for my own show.

I learned some useful things about story structure but once I discovered what the job of a screenwriter actually entailed, I put screenwriting on my Not To Do list. It is a very different career and although some authors write books *and* screenplays; it is a rare writer who succeeds at both. So now, I say "no" to screenwriting.

Other things on my Not To Do list:

- Text interviews. I save my writing for my own books and blog.

- Speaking engagements in person — unless it is at a location I want to travel to or an audience I don't already reach.

- Speaking in person or online on a topic that doesn't interest me.

- Meetings and webinars after six pm UK time with rare exceptions, for example, the live Ask ALLi Podcast I do with Orna Ross

- Writing books outside genres I love to read (which I learned when I helped my mum write sweet romance!)

- Foreign language self-publishing if there is no easy avenue for marketing. I have some non-fiction books in German which are in KU and have Amazon auto-ads on so they don't require any maintenance. But I much prefer to license foreign rights.

- Consulting or coaching.

- Video, unless it is entirely necessary. I stopped doing YouTube videos and Facebook Live a few years back as it is just too much work. I am now audio and voice-first.

- Amazon Ads and marketing data analysis. I outsource ads for non-fiction.

- Social media messages. I have an auto-reply to messages on Facebook which says I don't check them. I haven't checked LinkedIn for years, and I ignore messages on most services. The Contact page on my website is easy to find.

By saying no and setting boundaries, I free myself up to do the things only I can do, that I enjoy and which are the best use of my time. What could you say no to?

* * *

Mark: It's difficult to say no when you are first beginning, because often you need to try things out and feel them out to see if they are a good fit for you. **Sometimes you have to try something in order to K-N-O-W that it's a N-O.**

Also, early on, you're often desperate to be 'in demand' and are likely to say yes a lot.

That's okay.

Over time, you'll figure out what things work best for you, and which things don't. And you can then fall into a relaxed response to queries, demands, and requests.

I say no to most of the text interviews that come in for me, because I see it as me creating content for someone else's blog, website, or magazine. I will make an exception if the audience is right for me, or large enough, or, if it's an opportunity to earn a certain amount of money. Although in most of these cases it's not.

An audio or video interview is easier because often all I have to do is be available for a specified time where I'm answering questions. Most of the time, I don't have to prepare like a presentation or a pre-write. I can just ad lib and provide valuable content based on my own experiences and perspectives.

In that type of medium, they hear my voice, or they see me on a video. And that re-enforces my brand as a human, a real person, which is important to me. I enjoy the experience, and it takes very little of my time and energy.

After working with my publicist for less than six months, he now knows there are certain things I won't do, certain leads I won't take. He recognizes that they're not worth my time.

And, while I love helping authors, I'm all about helping authors understand the business of publishing. But I have no patience or aptitude for teaching them the craft of writing. I don't get any intrinsic reward from that, so will say no to money-making opportunities that are about the craft. It's just not a good fit.

I also say no to the things that take me more time than the reward that comes out of it. Placing those boundaries and restrictions has allowed me to embrace a much more relaxed approach in my daily writing life.

It's critical for authors to also say no to ideas.

One thing non-writers don't understand is that it's often not a lack of ideas we deal with. It's a lack of time to ever get all those ideas out into a piece of writing.

At first, worrying about all those ideas that you're not using can be overwhelming. But in order to adopt a relaxed author mindset, you need to allow yourself to say no to plenty of ideas. And sometimes, some of those ideas come back, days, months, or years later, in a different form, and in a way that works even better for you as a writer.

Just this morning, as I was walking upstairs to my den with my coffee, I had an idea that I had said no to by the time I reached the top of the stairs. It was intriguing but wouldn't fit with the project I was working on. Then, a few minutes later, when I was sitting down in front of my laptop, that fresh idea reminded me of an idea I had for something perhaps a dozen years ago that I had pushed away and never used.

But this time, when that old idea returned to me, it was during the right project, and I was able to incorporate it in. When it comes to saying no to brilliant creative ideas in your writing, sometimes saying no is really just postponing saying yes when the time or project is right.

* * *

"I've let go of the idea that I must work more hours to get better results. Ironically, I've been much more relaxed and I have more free time since I added 20 minutes or so each week where I look over what I've been doing and ask myself why and what results I'm achieving. If I don't have a good answer I stop doing it."

Lisa M. Lilly

"Deciding to not do ALL the things makes me a relaxed author. I don't really enjoy social media, so I have to choose carefully where I spend my time online and focus on being authentic on one or two platforms instead of trying to be everywhere all the time."

Kiersten Lillis

Resources:

- *Anything You Want: 40 Lessons for a New Kind of Entrepreneur* — Derek Sivers
- *Productivity for Authors: Find Time to Write, Organize Your Author Life, and Decide What Really Matters* — Joanna Penn

4.4 Organize and improve your processes

> "How we spend our days is of course how we spend our lives."
>
> Annie Dillard, *The Writing Life*

Mark: Understanding and accepting how you best work is critical for becoming a relaxed author.

I learned, years ago, that I work best to deadline. Whether it's a contract signed with a publisher, or an agreed-upon timeline with an editor, cover designer, or narrator, they all work best for me.

So, getting something in writing, or even publishing a book for pre-order, provides me that forced deadline that allows me to get and stay in the proper flow as a writer.

In daily process improvements, for me, **time-blocking and scheduling is important.** It might start with recognizing your own biorhythms and when you're most creative or analytical.

In the early mornings, I'm in that state of consciousness where I'm more in tune with the muse or whatever metaphysical thing that is. Over the years I've recognized that's when I'm going to get the most efficient writing done.

Sometimes I can push through the entire morning in that state, provided I have nothing else scheduled. But often it's the afternoons where I'll schedule more administrative or business-oriented writing tasks.

Ever since I blocked times in my calendar to leverage those times when I work best in different modes, I've become more efficient. And with that efficiency comes reduced stress about the projects I'm working at.

* * *

Joanna: Everyone is different. My creative and business processes will be different to yours, but what remains the same is the fact that you have to have processes in place if you want to run a successful business. For example, how you write and edit your books, how you publish, and how you market.

Your most effective processes will emerge over time, so don't worry if you haven't nailed them yet, or if you're still making tweaks. Here are some of the things that I have improved over the years.

I (usually) write fiction in a different location to where I write non-fiction. I've written several novels in the London Library, and in Boston Tea Party café in Bath, and now I write in a co-working space.

During the pandemic lockdowns, I managed the separation using playlists — an instrumental *Game of Thrones* soundtrack for my fiction, and rain and thunderstorms for non-fiction. This separation helps me 'change heads' so I can more easily write as J.F. Penn.

I schedule my time with Google Calendar, sometimes months in advance. I have time blocks for writing and editing, as well as recording and podcast production, meetings and admin, and personal time for exercise. My morning is usually creative and my afternoon is for business and marketing.

I outsource tasks that I can't do — or that it's not a good use of my time as covered in chapter 3.8. You can't do everything yourself if you want to run a successful author business. Find professionals you can trust and pay them on time, and you will build a team to help you improve your business.

Essentially, it all comes down to time management. Block out time for what you value, eliminate or outsource the other tasks, and you will achieve your goals.

* * *

Here are some ways that these authors improved their processes

"Setting business hours (a.k.a. making sure I had scheduled TIME OFF from all things related to my work, including social media) was a huge game-changer for me. Additionally, giving myself permission to go against the current indie 'best practice' of spending a lot of time, money and energy on ads and instead find my own way to grow my business changed my relationship with the 'business' side of my business drastically. I've found an approach that excites and inspires me on multiple levels and let go (mostly) of the idea that there's one right way to get to where I want to be."

Ember Casey

"I get my needed hours of sleep and I've followed your advice. I use a rain app with ear buds. I changed my writing location from where I do my day job, and I have scheduled work blocks just dedicated to writing. They've worked like a charm."

K.K. Johns

"I made a space to write. It's very small but dedicated to book work. I have a ritual every time I start: organize the space so it's clutter-free, make tea, pull the book's playlist, and read the last chapter."

Sierra Glass

"I compartmentalize. I separate my creative self from my business self from my self-care self. When I'm wearing my creative hat, I know I can relax and immerse myself in the story without worrying about uploads or marketing, etc. When I'm in marketing mode, I focus completely on that and put my creative brain away for a few hours each day. I also recognize that I need self-care, so I limit work hours to 40 hours per week and I make sure I'm exercising, spending time with my family, and doing the things I enjoy. Otherwise, what's the point?"

Nikita Slater

Resources:

- *Productivity for Authors: Find Time to Write, Organize Your Author Life, and Decide What Really Matters* — Joanna Penn
- *Deep Work: Rules For Focused Success in a Distracted World* — Cal Newport

4.5 Use tools to make your process more efficient

Joanna: Technology and tools allow us to leverage our time in order to spend more of it creating and less time on all the other stuff. Here are some of the main things I use but of course, you won't need all of them!

> Find what you need when you need it and use tools to make your author life easier.

Writing and editing: Scrivener for first draft writing and ProWritingAid as part of my editing process.

Formatting: Vellum to format ebooks.

Book marketing: Publisher Rocket for keywords and category research. Buffer for social media scheduling. Canva for image creation. Bookfunnel for delivery of ebooks and audiobooks.

Website: WordPress for my sites with various plugins. Payhip for direct sales of ebooks and audiobooks.

Email management: It's hard to imagine when you're just starting out, but there will come a time when email from fans and followers gets too much and you need some kind of solution both to send email and to manage incoming messages.

I use ConvertKit as my email service.

For management of email on TheCreativePenn, I use a FAQ page and an email form, rather than providing my email address on my website. This reduces spam and I also direct the form to my virtual assistant, Alexandra. She filters out the email I need to answer personally, and people on my email list have my direct email, anyway.

Time management: I use Google Calendar and Calendly for appointments

Accounting: Xero for invoicing and bank statement reconciliation as well as managing accounts.

This is not a complete list and the tools I use change over time. Most of them have free or reasonably priced options, but there are monthly charges once your business grows.

> You can find more of my recommended tools and tutorials at
> www.TheCreativePenn.com/tools

* * *

Mark: The relaxed author realizes they have only so much time and they don't stress out over how much time they've wasted. They recognize a good investment in a tool.

Not all tools work the same. And they often require an initial investment that might seem like you are back-tracking. But when you have adapted long-term thinking for your author career, you'll likely find that initial investment is worth it in the long run.

Different tools in varying situations are going to remove aspects you don't enjoy working on, that you don't like understanding. I remember learning how to hand-code an ePub using HTML in 2009, back in those early days of digital publishing, because I wanted to understand how they worked.

It was useful for me to understand how an ePub works. But I now use a combination of free and paid conversion tools that are easily available.

(Rather than repeat any of the tools Joanna covers, I'll try to share tools she didn't cover. But I do want to note that I also use and recommend several of the same tools she mentions.)

I leverage a combination of **Microsoft Excel** and **Google Sheets** for numerous tracking tasks related to my book catalog, planning the chapter breakdown of a book, and in collaborative writing projects.

One of the earliest examples of leveraging a spreadsheet comes from tracking manuscript submissions.

I would outline the name of a story, the genre, and the markets I had submitted them to. I would note the date I sent the submission out, when (or even if) the response came back, what that response was, and when and where the story was first published. I would continue to use the spreadsheet to track reprint sales of a story.

I can go back to the spring of 1989 when I first started effectively tracking my story submissions in a **Duo Tang** brand loose-leaf binding folder and see my submission and publication history for numerous short stories.

Looking at that Duo Tang, which I used until 2008, I can see that I mailed a horror story called "New Mix" along with an **SAE** (self-addressed stamped envelope) and an **IRC** (International Reply Coupon—it allows for the redemption of foreign post office stamps) to *Weird Tales* magazine. I received my rejection for that one rather quickly. My rejection slip came on May 23rd of that year.

I can also see that on September 15, 1990, after many submissions and rejections on a dozen or so other stories, I heard back from a magazine called *Chapter One* that they were interested in publishing my YA humor story "The Progressive Sidetrack" and would send me a contract for it within 90 days.

I received the contract on Oct 11th of that year and returned it, and a brief biography, the next day.

Being a young and panicked writer who didn't understand the glacial speed of publishing, I phoned the editor on Feb 6, 1991, worried that the signed contract had gone missing, because I hadn't heard back from the editor. (I later, of course, learned that you don't phone editors)

On August 17, 1991, I mailed a query about the status of "The Progressive Sidetrack" to the editor and publisher of *Chapter One*.

On September 27, 1991, I received a reply from the editor informing me that the story would appear in their October 1991 edition of the digest-sized magazine.

On December 9th I received a request from the editor of *Chapter One* for any updated author bio information. Publishing delays ended up pushing back that issue from October until late December. (I was beginning to more fully understand the typical snail-like speed of traditional publishing).

On September 30, 1992, my contributor's copy of the issue of *Chapter One* with my story "The Progressive Sidetrack" arrived in the mail.

I never would have remembered any of those details, but the original hand-written journal allows me to go back and trace the history of submissions, publications, and other correspondence. In 2008 I did similar tracking in a combination of spreadsheets (**Google Sheets**) and text documents (**Google Docs**).

For basic writing tools, such as the software that I use when I write, I've purchased, tried, and looked at several different ones over the years, like **Scrivener**. But for numerous reasons, I've found it easier to just keep falling back to **Microsoft Word**.

It's a program I've used the longest and am most comfortable with.

- Hundreds of my short stories and book file projects are already in MS Word.
- Most of the editors I work with as an indie author use MS Word with the 'Track Changes' option that we already know how to use.

- The traditional publishers I work with require MS Word format manuscripts.

- I can easily get a print-ready PDF file generated from MS Word using templates I've customized for myself over the years.

- Most of the free and paid ePub conversion tools accept or even require a .doc or .docx format.

I know that many other amazing pieces of software out there can help me be more efficient with other aspects of writing, but I find it far more comfortable — and less stressful — to fall back on MS Word.

Another tool I have recently adapted into my writing is **ProWritingAid**. It's a great way to help me find and catch issues and other basic problems before the manuscript goes to an editor for a line edit. It reduces the time (and cost) an editor is likely to have to spend on my manuscript.

When it comes to marketing (and, admittedly, this is both for my writing and for my podcast), I quite enjoy using **Headliner**, which allows for quick and effective audio sharing in a visual and animated medium. You upload your audio, there is built-in AI transcription, and within just a few minutes you can export direct to social media, or direct download a file that has your audio, transcribed, and with a customized size and shape and an audio wave that captures the eye in a 'newsfeed' page within platforms like Twitter or Facebook.

Speaking of marketing, since it regularly involves making temporary price changes and booking third-party newsletter ads, I'm a huge fan of the fact that platforms like Apple Books Author, Draft2Digital, Google Play Books Partner Center, and Kobo Writing Life all have payment scheduling tools where an author can set the start and end date of a price promotion (scheduling a price drop on a book from $4.99 USD to $0.99 USD for example) well ahead of time. A tool like this reduces a lot of stress and anxiety.

Unfortunately, the big player, Kindle Direct Publishing, doesn't offer this (except for limited windows within your KDP Select exclusivity 90 day periods), which means if you are wide, you need to plan on making the price drop anywhere from six to twelve hours prior to the day you want the price to change, and cross your fingers and hope it gets through at the right time.

I have found **BookBrush** an extremely efficient and timesaving way to create ads. With built-in automated tools to get marketing images for your book in various settings, automated and customized and modifiable templates with the specifications for BookBub and Facebook Ads, you can create beautiful and effective marketing images within minutes.

I use Draft2Digital's **Universal Book Links** (via **Books2Read.com**) for both my indie published and traditionally published books. Not only do they include all the major retailers and several library systems, but the links are geo-targeted so that customers in different countries are routed to the appropriate international storefronts for Amazon, Kobo, Google, and Apple.

Draft2Digital's Books2Read links allow for vanity URL creation (for example, Books2Read.com/publishingsuccess), making it easier to share links verbally for radio and podcast interviews. And you can have your Amazon, Apple, Google, and other affiliate codes embedded within the links, allowing an easy way to maximize your multiple revenue streams.

I also started leveraging my free **Author Page** on Books2Read. It's basically similar to the Amazon **Author Central** page, but it's not a single retailer and comes with additional flexibility to add links to your website, your social media, and custom carousels of your titles. I like to think of it being like **Author Central** but for all the retailers in a single spot.

Draft2Digital also has an **Account Sharing** option that is stress-free, because it allows me to assign limited access to update my titles, for example, to a virtual assistant. It's a secure way to leverage third-party support without giving someone access to my financial data. (Apple Books Author and Google Play also offer this option).

Another Draft2Digital tool I have started using since it launched in late 2020 is their **Payment Splitting** option. I have no less than a half-dozen collaboration projects, and more coming. The beauty of this tool is that Draft2Digital handles all the US tax forms directly with each contributor, and not only does the appropriate calculations on the payment split involved, but pays everybody automatically during the regular payment cycles for the platforms they distribute to. I don't need to take the money in, then run complex calculations and figure out ways to transfer money to my contributors. As a Canadian, operating with mostly US-based self-publishing platforms, I lose money on the USD to CAD conversion as the money comes in, then lose a little bit more on converting back to USD, or to GBP or some other currency where my contributors might live. Not to mention the time and hassle (and anxiety) of that process. Now, I don't even need to think about it. That's definitely relaxing.

And I am a huge fan of **ScribeCount** for saving time in keeping track of my sales on various platforms. Using a browser extension, I can see my sales across all major online platforms. There is even now an option for me to input (or upload) sales from outside the regular channels, including traditional publishing, direct sales, and other sources of writing-related income. The reporting presents dynamic and easy to decipher charts and graphs to help me easily see which of my titles are selling on what platforms or methods, and what my split is. For a wide publishing author, this easily saves hours of time.

One of the most basic and effective free tools I've adapted into my writing life is leveraging my calendar for actual writing. I use **Google Calendar**, which is synced to my phone and to the various Google Home devices in our house.

And I block specific segments of time with a note of what writing project I'm going to be working on. It might seem like a basic or simple tool, but the process of blocking those times, and being able to look at my calendar and know that, tomorrow, for example, I'm going to be working for one and a half hours on the novel *Fright Nights, Big City*. I can mentally prepare myself for that task, so that when I am at my desk with a fresh cup of coffee and open my laptop, I have already done a lot of subconscious pre-processing of what I'll be writing.

Back-up tools can save you tremendous anxiety

While we're talking about tools, software, and hardware that will make an author more relaxed, one thing we should note is the importance of either automated or manual processes of backing up your work. Nothing can be more frustrating to a writer than losing endless hours of writing or editing when some glitch in their computer system fails, or is lost, or stolen.

Leveraging backups — even multiple or redundant backups — is an effective way to continue working with peace of mind that if something terrible happens, all your hard work is not entirely lost.

Here are a list of potential backup tools you can consider using:

- Hardware options — An external USB hard drive.
- Online options — Dropbox, OneDrive, Google Drive
- Automated backup programs/subscriptions — Carbonite, HDClone

In the resources below is a link to a summer 2021 article from *LiveWire* that reviews and shares pros and cons of 32 of the best free back-up software tools.

* * *

"As an independent publisher, I found the final preparation of ebook and paperback files for uploading to be the most stressful task. I now have Vellum, which takes all the angst out of what was previously the most hair-pulling task. I love that there are now so many great tools available to help with tasks like formatting, editing, cover creation, etc. They not only help reduce stress levels, but also enable the production of professional end products."

Alicia Hope

Resources:

- List of tools and tutorials for writers by Joanna Penn — www.TheCreativePenn.com/tools

- Scrivener for writing and plotting/organizing — www.TheCreativePenn.com/scrivenersoftware

- ProWritingAid for editing — www.TheCreativePenn.com/prowritingaid

- Vellum for ebook and print formatting — www.TheCreativePenn.com/vellum

- Publisher Rocket — www.TheCreativePenn.com/rocket

- Buffer social media scheduling — www.buffer.com

- Canva image creation — www.canva.com

- Bookfunnel for delivery of ebooks and audiobooks — www.Bookfunnel.com

- Payhip for direct sales — www.Payhip.com

- ConvertKit for email management — www.TheCreativePenn.com/convert

- Example FAQ page — www.TheCreativePenn.com/faq
- Example form for email — www.TheCreativePenn.com/contact
- There are lots of forms you can use depending on your website. Joanna uses Gravity Forms — www.gravityforms.com
- Calendly for scheduling — www.calendly.com
- Xero for invoicing and accounting — www.xero.com
- ScribeCount — www.markleslie.ca/scribecount
- Headliner for audio sharing — www.headliner.app
- BookBrush for book ads — www.BookBrush.com
- Universal Book Links — www.Books2Read.com
- Draft2Digital payment splitting — www.draft2digital.com/blog/announcing-d2d-payment-splitting/

- 32 Best Free Backup Software Tools: Reviews of the best free backup software for Windows. *LiveWire*, July 1, 2021 — www.lifewire.com/free-backup-software-tools-2617964

4.6 Find voices you trust and tune out the rest

Mark: One of the best things about being a writer today is that there is so much information out there, much of it freely available. That, of course, might also be one of the worst things about being a writer.

All of that info can be overwhelming. Figuring out how to sift through and make sense of it can cause much anxiety in an author's life.

It's that careful curation, developed over time, and over experimentation and taking a perhaps 'Goldilocks' approach, which I will explain below, that reduces the anxiety.

Because that information, and the things we need to learn to continue to grow and develop as writers, never stops.

Whether you are just starting in your writing career, or have been doing it for a long time, there will always be something to learn, someone to learn from, and new opportunities and options to explore.

Along with that will be voices sharing their ways of 'how to do it.' So many voices. So many choices. So many options.

Here's how I apply a 'Goldilocks Principle' to the voices and the methodologies, and the options I'm presented with.

In the classic fable of that young girl and the three bears, she tried from three different bowls of porridge, sitting in three different chairs, and sleeping in three different beds. It's a simplistic tale, but her process allowed her to try each out and determine what the best fit for her was.

There might, of course, be some cases where your internal radar or instincts might immediately tell you that something is definitely not for you. That's okay.

Trust your instinct. You have developed it for a reason.

But experimenting and trying, or at least briefly tasting, one dish, allows you to know if it's a fit for you, something you're comfortable with, and it reduces a significant stressor in the indie author community: the FOMO that haunts us.

We all see authors doing something — likely because a guru out there did it and found success and is now selling that idea to other authors — and we don't want to miss catching that wave. You might have anxiety from never testing or trying something. So sometimes, just trying it, allows you to know, beyond instinct, if it's for you or not.

But only you can truly know if some advice, some information, some strategy, some tactic, is going to sit well with you.

Oprah Winfrey said, "If it feels right, I do it. If it feels wrong, I don't. You've got to be willing to take your chances doing stuff that may look crazy to other people—or not doing something that looks right to others, but feels wrong to you."

Whenever I'm looking at advice, suggestions, and 'how-to' approaches, I often pause to take in that information with a grain of salt. Meaning, I accept and attend to it while maintaining a degree of optimistic skepticism about its truth.

I consider the source. What perspective is that advice coming from? How is their situation, their experience, their own specific writing (genre, format, etc.) different than my own? What other factors are at play that might not be evident at face value? What is their motive for sharing this information? How might I apply or adapt that information, if I find it useful and applicable to me?

Something else I have learned is adapted from Michael Connelly's Harry Bosch, a detective who seeks justice for any victim, regardless of who they are, their gender, race, class, position in society.

Everybody counts, or nobody counts.

I repeat that mantra in my mind often when I'm at an event, when I'm about to begin a talk to a room full of writers, regardless of the size or experience level of the audience.

To me, it's important to recognize that, even as I'm about to address a large crowd, there are likely writers with far more experience, skill, knowledge, and perspective in that audience that I can learn from. But there's not a single person in that room that I can't learn **something** from. Yes, even that writer who hasn't yet written their first story has something valuable to share. They bring something fresh and completely unique that I'm sure I can benefit from if I'm open to attending and listening.

It's a reminder that, as much as I've learned, and continued to learn over the years, as many mentors and teachers and instructors I've benefited from, that process of listening and learning will never stop.

While I don't take all advice and information at face value, I apply, as I mentioned, that proverbial grain of salt, I also don't immediately dismiss anything that is coming from a different perspective than mine.

And, ultimately, I remind myself that no single answer, no single solution, no single bit of advice or suggestion, or path, is going to be the same for everyone.

Us authors are very much like unique snowflakes in our approach, our strategy, our method, our intrinsic and extrinsic motivations. Embrace those differences, even the subtle ones, and trust your instincts, relishing in the fact that your path, like your writing itself, is unique and constantly growing, constantly evolving.

* * *

Joanna: The online world is a noisy place with lots of rabbit holes you can potentially fall down. Different people will tell you that different things work — or don't work — in every area of writing craft, publishing, marketing and author business. Of course, Mark and I are just two more of those people offering advice. (Sorry!)

You need to learn from others on the author journey.

It would be crazy not to, since most of us share our experience hoping to help others save time, money and heartache. But you need to find a way to filter out the voices that don't work for you and pay attention to those people who make sense for your situation.

This will be different for everyone.

Here are some questions I use to filter my influences.

Does this person do what I want to do — and have they been doing it successfully for longer than I have?

For example, I enjoy books by Stephen King and he's been writing for around sixty years, so I am definitely going to pay attention to his thoughts on the craft.

But as much as I love King, I am not going to pay any attention to his thoughts on self-publishing or book marketing or even building an author career. He started out at a very different time and he has a long history within traditional publishing and many people who do marketing for him.

On the other hand, I follow Kristine Kathryn Rusch and Dean Wesley Smith because they have been writing and publishing nearly as long as King, but they also embrace indie publishing and keep pushing the boundaries of what's possible for their books.

I learn from other people about other topics. For example, I learned from Yaro Starak about blogging and podcasting, Brian Clark about online business, and Orna Ross about creativity and community.

How can I learn from the people I choose?

Many authors have non-fiction books. If you haven't read *On Writing* by Stephen King, go get it now! If you need to learn something, there will probably be a book on it, and writers are readers first, so start there.

Then check what else they have. Kristine Kathryn Rusch and Dean Wesley Smith have non-fiction books for authors as well as online courses that go into craft and business. They also write regular blog posts and Kris has a Patreon where you can get her business articles early. You can also see them speak at various conferences in person, and I have traveled from the UK to Oregon twice and also to Las Vegas for their events.

Some authors offer 1:1 coaching, group consulting, or masterminds where you can get more personalized help. Just check their website to see what they offer.

Does what they teach resonate with me and fit with my lifestyle and goals at this point in my author journey?

Trust your feelings and your instinct, which will develop over time as you become more confident on your author journey.

For example, I've read many books and taken several courses on plotting. I have tried so hard to become a plotter — but I am a discovery writer, and now I embrace that. It doesn't matter how many people tell me I 'should' do it a different way, it doesn't work for me — and that's okay.

As another example, I love posting pictures on Instagram @jfpennauthor, so I took an online course on improving my Instagram presence.

I hated the course, not because it was bad, but because I love my Instagram as a personal place for fun rather than business. So I gave up the course and haven't implemented any of the tips.

None of these books or courses or people teaching them were 'wrong,' they just weren't right for me on my author journey.

You also have to decide what's right for you at a particular time.

Many authors overwhelm themselves with information on publishing and book marketing before even finishing the first draft. Don't do that! Finish the book and learn what you need just in time.

* * *

"I stay relaxed by taking my time, focusing on my art, and blocking out all the voices telling me I have to do a ton of stuff that will probably just distract me. I think you need to learn to filter out a lot of the advice that people bombard you with. Some of it is helpful, but a lot of it will only send your stress levels through the roof."

E.P. Clark

"Being informed by people I trust. Choosing carefully who I listen to so I don't get swamped by information. I choose quality over quantity of voices. Not with the aim of only listening to those I agree with (different views are good) but I need to curate and manage my input streams."

Molly Matheson

Resources:

- *On Writing: A Memoir of the Craft*
  — Stephen King

- Books for authors by Dean Wesley Smith and Kristine Kathryn Rusch
  — www.wmgpublishinginc.com/writers/

- Kris Rusch's Business articles on Patreon
  — Patreon.com/kristinekathrynrusch

4.7 Learn about money

Please note: We are not financial or legal advisors and this is not financial or legal advice.

Joanna: It was November 2011, and we sat in the one-bedroom basement flat we rented in London. We had downsized in order to reduce expenses and get rid of our debt. I had given up my well-paid consulting job, and we had sold our three-bedroom house and investments in Australia so I could try to make a living with my writing.

What a crazy idea!

My husband, Jonathan, had a job, but we had taken a *serious* drop in household income and standard of living.

"We need to set up our UK pensions," Jonathan said. "We should also start putting money into ISAs." (Tax-efficient investment products similar to a US IRA).

I promptly burst into tears.

The thought of trying to find money to invest was overwhelmingly stressful. My decision to leave my job had decimated our household income. I was worried about paying the rent, let alone investing for the future. I also didn't know how to set up a pension and I didn't understand how ISAs worked. I was embarrassed by my lack of knowledge.

A decade later and we both manage our own SIPPs (Self-Invested Pension Plan) and ISAs. We read Money Week and the Financial Times and we are well on the way to financial independence (FI). I've even been on the Choose FI Podcast to talk about my money journey, and I've included my list of recommended money books and podcasts for you below.

Because education is the key to reducing stress around money.

It's like a new language. You have to put in the initial time to learn how it works — as well as change your mindset — but once the proverbial penny drops, everything becomes much easier.

I no longer weep at the idea of investments. In fact, I enjoy investing and actively manage my money — now and for the future.

If you want to be a more relaxed author about money, then take the time to learn about it.

Keep seeking out more information in whatever form you prefer until money no longer scares you.

At first it may all sound like gobbledegook, especially if you come from a family (like mine) where money was not discussed.

But at some point, you will read something or listen to something that makes sense for you. You can take action and then life really does change.

* * *

Mark: Even when you're not consciously thinking about it, money can have a dramatic impact on you. It can be subconsciously stressing you out without you even realizing it.

In the same way that you have to understand and accept your own processes for creativity and writing, you have to look at, learn, and acknowledge your own relationship with money.

It's not always easy, and facing the way you interact with money can be extremely stressful, frustrating, and challenging. But understanding it is half of the battle.

Over the years, I've tracked the way I interact with money and determined some consistent patterns in the way I spend. Some of them are not healthy. I have learned ways to avoid putting myself in situations where I am more likely to make money-related decisions that are not good for me in the long term.

For example, if I'm walking around with cash in my wallet, I'm more likely to make a purchase without thinking twice. But if I have to use my bank card or a credit card to make a payment, there's an additional barrier of a slightly more complex transaction taking place — one that comes with additional considerations regarding bank balance and the use of credit — that create just enough resistance to allow me to reflect a bit deeper on whether I should make that purchase or investment.

One of the most profound resources that helped me come to terms with my relationship with money was David Chilton's *The Wealthy Barber*. "A dollar saved is two dollars earned," is one principle from this book that advises investing ten percent of all your earnings for successful and guaranteed long-term growth.

It was the anecdotal story and how Chilton rolled the tale out that resonated with me. And while I wish that I had applied that to my relationship with money at a much earlier age, I also don't fret. I can't change the past, but I can change my present, and my future. Remember that adage: the best time to plant a tree was twenty-years ago. The second-best time is now.

Resources:

- List of recommended money books and podcasts
— www.TheCreativePenn.com/moneybooks

- Joanna Penn on the Choose FI Podcast
— www.ChooseFI.com/the-creative-penn/

- *The Wealthy Barber: Everyone's Common Sense Guide to Becoming Financially Independent* — David Chilton

4.8 Look after your physical and mental health

Mark: While there are core basic recommendations about behaviors and habits to maintain a healthy body, everyone is going to have their own approach to it. I think it's important to learn from the experts while trusting your own body. Our bodies tell us things regularly. Some of them are subtle, and others are blatant. It's critical that we listen to both medical and health experts as well as what our bodies are saying.

I have found that engaging in physical and non-cerebral activities have the effect of benefiting both my peace of mind and my body.

High blood pressure is something I was cursed with genetically. It runs in the family, and I've struggled with it since I was in my mid-twenties. For the longest time, I was able to maintain a relatively healthy blood pressure via lifestyle choices: monitoring what I ate and drank, how much I slept, my body weight, and the amount of exercise. This worked well until I reached my mid-forties, and none of those activities worked as effectively.

For almost two decades, I put off taking medication for high blood pressure. I had been on medication for epilepsy since I was five years old and was only able to come off my meds in my mid-twenties. (Yes, I realize how absolutely fortunate I am to do that. Most people with epilepsy are never that lucky). But, having spent most of my time on this planet with no choice but taking medication in order to live a normal life, there was a mental block in the idea of starting some other medication.

But the stats on my blood pressure readings kept climbing. And I had to come to terms with the fact that if I didn't start taking mediation, I could end up having a stroke.

Now, with a combination of monitoring my diet, weight, sleep, and exercise, along with my medication, I can maintain a normal or only slightly elevated blood pressure.

Long walks and long runs — either with a book to listen to or, sometimes, completely technology-free — have a dramatic impact on both my physical and mental state. I have found, for example, that immediately after a long run, or playing squash, or some other physical exercise, my blood pressure lowers. So regular exercise is part of the key to keeping it from getting elevated.

But those long excursions on foot, in particular, are also ideal for my mental well-being. I often work out plot and character developments in my head on those runs and walks. Or sometimes I'll see or hear something that sparks a fresh idea. So engaging in that physical activity is good for both my body and my mind.

I wear a **Fitbit** and, since 2016, have taken part in a weekly "Workweek Challenge" that a writer I met in Austin at the Smarter Artist Summit organizes for a bunch of us. There is a playful and fun competition to see how many steps about eight to ten other writers are taking between Monday and Friday each week, and seeing where I rank in the on-going step count is motivation to take the longer route, use the stairs instead of an elevator where I'm able, and put in just a few more kilometers. It's a reminder that I'm not alone — that like me, these other writers have an often sedentary life, and we're pushing one another to get just a few extra steps in each day. It benefits me in both my physical and mental health.

I have also learned that routines and keeping a clean and clutter-free workspace and email inbox are also subtle things that bring a deeper and more lasting peace of mind when I'm getting ready to write.

Similarly, because I no longer work in an office, which often requires additional steps, I have a home-made standing desk. I alternate between sitting at my regular desk and then standing. I've learned to write or edit while standing there, or even on our treadmill (using another home-made shelf that can easily support my laptop), and I do the majority of my virtual meetings, interviews and author coaching sessions while standing, since my laptop is at the top of the standing desk, its camera requires me to be standing in order to be seen.

For me, combining several incremental changes and small adaptations into my daily and weekly routine has made a huge and positive difference.

* * *

Joanna: As writers, we spend a lot of time in our heads — but **we are not just a brain with a pair of hands** to channel words onto the page. We have bodies and they need care and maintenance.

Like many writers and desk-workers, I ended up with back and shoulder pain, headaches and migraine, weight gain and other health issues. Once I hit my mid-thirties, I couldn't shake it off anymore, and I had to make changes for my long-term health. I covered this in detail in *The Healthy Writer*, which I co-wrote with Dr Euan Lawson, but the short version is:

If you don't look after your physical and mental health, your writing will suffer, as well as the quality of the rest of your life.

The great thing is that eating well and physical movement make you feel good — and more relaxed — so it's worth spending the time to figure out what you enjoy and what's sustainable for you. Once again, it doesn't have to be what someone else says is right. It's what works for you.

Start by removing stressors

My migraines disappeared once I stopped working in an open-plan office with constant noise and stimulation. My sleep improved when I removed noise and light with earplugs and an eye mask.

Find movement you love

I enjoy walking and lifting weights and I get outside into nature almost every day. We don't have a car, so I have a lot of extra movement built in and I wear an Apple Watch to make sure I break up sedentary periods and meet my movement goals every day.

Find a way of eating that works for you

I love my food — it's pleasure and reward, it's comfort and solace. I love cheese and chocolate and I enjoy drinking wine and gin & tonic. I've tried 'diets' but now I live an intermittent fasting lifestyle, which for me means I eat every day within a certain time period — unless it's a special occasion when I just do whatever I like!

These are all simple practices to maintain and make all the difference to my daily life — and keep me healthy and happy so I can create.

Sorting out your food and movement and sleep will certainly help with mental health, but we all move up and down the spectrum of what is 'normal' in our lives, so give yourself grace as life happens.

You will have to find what works for your health in all areas — and like writing, it's a lifelong journey. Your body and mind are yours to the grave, so look after them.

* * *

These writers also find movement important for being a relaxed author

"Movement is key. I make a point of getting away from my desk for physical activity on a daily basis. I rarely solve writing problems during exercise, but movement never fails to clear my brain and make whatever situation I'm wrestling with less stressful. I return to my desk clear-eyed and work more efficiently."

Nicole Burnham

"Solutions, often the very best solution, arise when you just walk away from a problem for a few hours or days. Meditation helps a lot, but that doesn't have to mean sitting on a zafu in a dojo. It might involve parking yourself on a sofa staring into space, or working in a garden — yours, a neighbour's, wherever. Just do something that engages the body and lets the mind's back-burner simmer away at your problem."

Kathy Mac

"Get outside, do exercise. That seems to help a lot. The fitter I am, the more I write."

Cathryn Hein

Resources:

- *The Healthy Writer: Reduce Your Pain, Improve Your Health, and Build a Writing Career for the Long Term* — Joanna Penn and Dr Euan Lawson

- *Fast, Feast, Repeat: The Comprehensive Guide to Delay, Don't Deny Intermittent Fasting* — Gin Stephens

- Intermittent Fasting Stories Podcast with Gin Stephens. Episode 155 is with Joanna Penn. On your favorite podcast app or www.intermittentfastingstories.com

4.9 Keep a long-term mindset

Joanna: Thinking long-term is critical if you want to be a relaxed author.

You can relax about writing when you know you have a lifetime to improve. Sure, do your best and work to deadline if you choose, but this one book doesn't have to be the pinnacle of your career. You will have other chances.

You can relax about publishing options when you understand copyright lasts for your lifetime and 50-70 years after you die. If you retain your rights and license selectively, you have time to make the most of your intellectual property.

You can relax about launching a book if you measure its success over years instead of weeks. You can relax about growing your email list when you understand that it will build slowly over time.

You can relax about making money as a writer when you have years to grow multiple streams of income — and you see that a decade makes an incredible difference in the opportunities that emerge for writers to make more money. How many more possibilities will there be in another decade?

Look at the writers ahead of you on the author journey and you will see how time plays a significant part in their success.

Everyone starts with nothing, but if you take a step every day in the direction you want to travel and navigate the inevitable changes along the way, you will achieve your goals.

Make sure to enjoy the journey, because the destination will always move further away. That's just human nature!

* * *

Mark: No pun intended, but it can take a long time to develop a long-term mindset. When something is causing you anxiety I've found that asking this question can be helpful: "Will this matter tomorrow, next week, next month, next year?" I know it's a simple question, but the simple questions sometimes give us the simplest peace of mind is.

Will this actually matter in the long run, in the big picture, in the grand scheme of things?

It's very urgent now or it's upsetting me now. But that question often helps me frame it better.

One thing I know many authors fall victim to is obsessively looking at their sales dashboards on a daily, or even hourly, basis. Yes, sometimes you are running a promotion and want to see and measure the effectiveness of those campaigns. But outside that, how healthy is it?

Assuming you've done all the hard and right work producing a great product that's targeted to the right audience, looking at your sales dashboard will not make sales happen.

Sometimes scheduling your time for a daily check-in, perhaps after you complete an important task that furthers your author career (like writing, or important admin or marketing work) is less stressful.

And also, when you look at it in a larger picture, over the course of weeks, months, and years, you can see the patterns more easily as opposed to focusing on just the negatives: Those days where there's a dip in sales, or perhaps even no sales at all.

It's like looking at average review rating as opposed to the one-star reviews.

I suppose I'm fortunate to have cut my chops on the traditional side of publishing and bookselling.

I credit my work in the book industry since the early '90s to recognize a couple of things. Selling is seasonal and cyclical, and bookstores lose money three-quarters of the year and make all their money in the last quarter of the year.

And because I started in traditional publishing, where you would mail a manuscript away and maybe six to nine months later you would get a rejection, most likely, or sometimes an acceptance (the ratio was often 13:1 respectively), I learned to consider the big picture and the long run.

I was fortunate to be pre-conditioned to think long term. So, when the option of indie publishing came along, it was a change in mindset to think short term. I was lucky in many ways that I had no choice but to wait. It helped precondition my patience, which allowed me to relax and recognize the long-term patterns.

When things aren't doing well in the present, I can acknowledge that "Yes, things are not working right now, but things come in waves." For example, vampires are hot, then they're not, then they're hot, then they're not, then they're hot in a completely different way.

All of these patterns, huge trends, and waves have constantly been an ongoing thing in the book industry. And if we focus only on the peaks and the valleys as opposed to looking at the normalization, we cause ourselves more stress than we need to.

* * *

"I have a long-term view and a global view. I know it doesn't matter if I put a book out and it doesn't sell well. Because I know from experience, some bad selling books can explode in certain countries and on certain platforms. I focus on creating intellectual property and having fun and I know my readers will come to me over time. Having fun is the most important thing for writers!"

Connor Whiteley

"The longer I've been in this business and the older I get, the stress has lessened. It could be that I'm more comfortable with the indie publishing process now, or it could be that I've shifted priorities… Sometimes we just have to let things go, relax a bit, and hit it again. There is always tomorrow (well, usually …)"

Maddie James

Resources:

- *The Successful Author Mindset: A Handbook for Surviving the Writer's Journey*
  — Joanna Penn

- *The 7 P's of Publishing Success*
  — Mark Leslie Lefebvre

How to remain a relaxed author

Joanna: Becoming — and remaining — a relaxed author is about **making a series of choices over your writing career, and in your wider life.**

A few years back, Jonathan and I decided to engineer our lives away from stress and actively make choices to reduce anxiety. Of course, there will always be challenges and there are also good types of stress, for example, walking ultra-marathons, which I do several times a year. But for our physical and mental health and happiness, we made — and continue to make — specific choices.

In my last months of working as an IT consultant back in 2011, I used to cry in the toilets because I was so miserable. I was wracked with migraines from the open plan environment and working too many hours on high-stress projects. My decision to work from home as an author entrepreneur reduced my stress dramatically and my migraines pretty much disappeared.

We sold our house and downsized to a one-bedroom rental, paying off all our debt so we could more easily control our finances on a reduced income.

We moved out of London to Bath in order to live somewhere quieter, where we could walk more in nature and live at a slower pace.

We don't own a car because driving in the UK is busy and stressful, and parking is terrible in Bath, anyway. We use public transport and also belong to a car club and rent by the hour or the occasional weekend.

We mainly use index funds for investment because it's a simple, low maintenance, long-term approach, while still reducing stress for the long term by having a pension/superannuation fund in place.

In terms of my writing life, I've gone into detail on lots of decisions in this book, and I have to keep reminding myself of them in order to remain a relaxed author.

There's enough to be stressed about in the world, without letting your writing be that thing. What decisions can you make that will help you become — and remain — a relaxed author?

* * *

Mark: One way I'm able to maintain an on-going relaxed perspective as an author is recognizing that **there are inevitably going to be fluctuations.** There will be things that bring me stress. Just because I prefer to be a relaxed author doesn't mean that I'm always relaxed.

I hope that by the time you've gotten to this point in the book you realize that, although Joanna and I are advocates for the benefits of being a relaxed author, neither of us is always relaxed; and occasionally we find ourselves frustrated, upset, angry, confused, or anxious.

It happens to all of us. And that's okay. Beating ourselves up for feeling a certain way, for acknowledging anxiety and stress in our lives, only compounds the effect it has on us.

Even if you establish ways to be more relaxed in your approach, you'll likely find yourself veering off in a less-relaxed direction from time to time. That's okay. It's part of the process of course correction. You veer off course, you make an adjustment to slowly return back.

There were times during the writing of this book where both Joanna and I experienced stress. One of the ways we reduced that anxiety was acknowledging, to the other person, what it was that caused that stress. Clear and consistent communication along the way played a role at reducing it while it was happening.

Another thing we quickly came to realize is that, though the two of us are quite similar in our perspectives and over-arching views of writing and publishing, we have unique ways we prefer to work. Communication of those preferences was important to ensure we could each fall into the roles that made us more comfortable, effective, and productive. Here, for example, Joanna took on more of a Project Manager role, outlining the tasks in order and the deadlines for each of them. Taking that role allowed her to relax. And, for me, being someone who works to deadline, having her step up and create a concrete outline was exactly what I needed in order to effectively apply myself to this project.

We each allowed one another to adapt the roles that best suited us. This allowed us to more fully enjoy the process of co-authoring.

Along the way, there were hiccoughs. Misunderstandings that meant re-working some previous work, ideas on changing some of the ways we had originally decided to roll this book out, and even health setbacks that temporarily delayed forward progress. So we communicated and altered our plan, our approach, and our expectations.

So, if, despite having leveraged some of what you've read in this book to become more relaxed, you find moments of anxiety, and tension, know that there's no way for us to be immune to it. We just have to **remember to continue to adapt and adjust, and to veer back onto that relaxed path.**

Conclusion

If you are not a relaxed author 100% of the time, don't worry, that's completely normal!

Life is a journey and you will inevitably face challenges along the way — those you choose and those that blindside you suddenly.

Writing is often the way we figure things out and process our pain and struggle, as well as enabling us to share our stories and what we learn.

> **Writing is sacred, so protect it from stress as much as possible, because you need it to navigate the path ahead.**

Start with this process.

(1) Pay attention to how you feel and identify when you are stressed or anxious about something.

(2) Consider what you could do to remove the stressor altogether or reduce its impact. Is it *really* necessary?

(3) Take action — and then circle back to paying attention to how you feel. Has the stress reduced? Are you more relaxed?

Only you can take steps to become a more relaxed author, and we hope this book has given you some ideas.

Happy writing!

Need more help?

Sign up for Joanna's *free* Author Blueprint and email series, and receive useful information on writing, publishing, book marketing, and making a living with your writing:

www.TheCreativePenn.com/blueprint

* * *

Sign up for the Stark Reflections on Writing and Publishing for no more than two monthly emails with links to trends, insights, and inspiration related to the business of writing and publishing:

www.starkreflections.ca/newsletter/

Love podcasts?

Join Joanna every Monday for The Creative Penn Podcast where she talks about writing, publishing, book marketing, and the author business.

Available on your favorite podcast app.

Find the backlist episodes at

www.TheCreativePenn.com/podcast

Every Friday Mark shares his on-going insights, learnings, and very frank reflections about the business of writing and publishing in his Stark Reflections on Writing and Publishing Podcast.

Subscribe via your favorite podcast app, or find episodes here:

www.starkreflections.ca

Appendix 1: More reasons why authors are NOT relaxed

There were many valuable insights from authors who responded to our June 2021 survey, so we have included selected quotes with permission from the authors.

These answers are in response to the question: **What makes you most stressed and anxious — and not relaxed! — about being an author?**

* * *

"Deadlines, pressure to perform, not writing enough, dying before I can tell all my stories but all the while my brain is stewing on the stories and they won't come out until fully formed but the clock is ticking and time is flying and there aren't enough hours in the day and each day slips by faster and faster, and where did they go and now

I have to get back to my WIP but my brain is still thinking… you know, that kind of thing."

Josh Kilen

"It is stressful and not at all helpful to maintain a productive mindset when one's daily priorities are at war with each other daily. The constant tug and shove between, writing and daily life chores is wearing. One is supposed to compartmentalize writing, marketing, research, household chores, family obligations, and outside interests, but that requires the discipline of a Jesuit monk and rarely works well. That daily feeling of thrashing about in a sea of 'I should be doing: I must do this: I have to get that done: Am I wasting my time?' is what triggers the stress and destroys inner peace."

Rick Grant

"Information overload in all areas. Feeling like I'm always behind because as soon as I learn something, algorithms change! Wanting to just write, but knowing that I need to keep up with marketing too. People trumpeting loudly about how we must do the next thing to stay viable."

Rachelle Christensen

"The feeling that I should be doing this thing and that thing and the other thing for marketing while also churning out dozens of books at high speed in order to compete commercially. The pressure to write commercial fiction if I want to be counted as a 'real' indie author. It feels like an unfriendly space for those of us who want to take more time and focus on our art. Yes, art.

I decided to try the indie path for the artistic freedom it offered me, but the culture around it seems to be one of high-pressure, high-speed, commercial production. If I'd wanted to be a factory worker, I would have worked in a factory."

E.P. Clark

"Trying to keep up with what others are doing, whether it's paying attention to a peer's word count, sales numbers, or amount of books they are putting out."

Zach Bohannon

"The uncertainty and isolation. Will this book sell? Am I making the right decision focusing on this series instead of my other series? Do I write what brings me joy, or what I think will sell? Do I try to combine both? Do I go wide or KU? Have I chosen the right branding to attract readers who get me?"

Gillian St. Kevern

"I am incredibly worried about making a mistake with my writing and equally worried I am making a mistake BY trying to write at all."

Sharon Markatcheff

"I am very new in my author journey and I worry about literally everything. Can I make it a viable career when I have so little time to write around two small children, should I self or traditional publish? With traditional, will an agent want it and then will a publisher? In self-publishing: how will I manage to juggle everything and do it professionally? Will I end up spending very scarce money to never see it again? Will people actually read my book and if they do, will they find it any good?

These things go round and round in my head until I feel like I'm going to have a panic attack and often take away the actual joy I get from writing. I want to be successful and yet sometimes the list of things I need to do paralyzes me."

Anonymous

"If there is one characteristic I see far too frequently among beginning writers it is a deep uncertainty and fear that can only be corrosively damaging and is perhaps the greatest barrier to any feeling of joy and satisfaction they might get out of their endeavours. I'd like to see your book combat that."

Rick Grant

"FOMO and terror I'm doing everything wrong every time I see someone do something different. That goes along with why I dislike being on social media so much — it's so hard not to compare what I'm doing to what other seemingly happier and more successful people are doing."

Anonymous

"Sometimes, checking the sales reports too often and not seeing my income increase how I hoped it would locks up my creative energy and makes me fixate on the data instead. Data is great, but agonizing over it at the cost of producing - writing - only compounds the problem and piles on the stress."

Mana Sol

"The number of things indie authors are expected to be able to master, not just writing the book but building up a social media following, selling dealing with rights etc."

Lottie Clark

"The need to keep up with the on-going spinning of writing, publishing, and marketing causes me a huge amount of anxiety. I'm afraid that if I stop running, I'll never start again; or that if I slow down I'll fall behind — even though I know there is no one to fall behind because I'm the only one running in the race. Nothing about my author life is relaxed."

Jeff Elkins

"Not being able to allocate enough time to writing/marketing. Before setting out on the path to being an author, I had no idea how much post writing work there would be. I knew there would be some editing and formatting, but not how much. The biggest surprise has been how much effort has gone into marketing (website, social media, email lists, adverts, etc)."

Mark Probert

"The overwhelm of how much there is to learn, I write non-fiction so not so much about craft, but formatting, where/how to publish, advertising… you know all the things!! Plus, you ask a question on an indie author FB group/page and you get conflicting answers, and still don't know what to do. The loneliness and having no one who understands to discuss ideas/thoughts with."

Sheila Lamb

"Fear of being judged stops me from being a relaxed author. I know that if we put our work out there, then we have to expect anyone and everyone to have an opinion on it and readers are, of course, entitled to leave their thoughts in a review. However, I don't want to know what they think and so I don't read them. I have professionals whose opinions I value and trust to tell me the truth about my books. If ever I stray from this rule and read a review, be it good or bad, it can wobble my confidence for days, and sometimes longer. Avoiding them is the most stressful part of my job."

Imogen Clark

"Feelings of pressure and failure, which come from things like: endless talk about rapid release, or getting a new book out every month (vital!). Amazon exclusivity (vital!). Six-figure success (vital!). Writing to market (vital!)."

Charlotte E. English

"Feeling limited. I often feel that I get a lot of advice about how I should only write one genre, series vs stand-alones, tropes to adhere to, etc., and it can all start to feel a bit overwhelming. I started writing because there are so many stories I want to tell, but at the end of the day it seems I can only afford to keep doing so if I accept and embrace some limitations. As someone with wide-ranging creative interests this can be truly dispiriting and make it hard to remember why I fell in love with writing in the first place."

H.B. Reneau

"The idea of a hard launch date gives me hives. I've seen too many launches go wrong: pre-orders canceled; files not uploaded by vendors on time; third parties (formatters, cover designers, proofreaders, printers) dropping the ball at the last minute; tech glitches; disruptive world events. All those months of building buzz just to have the book trip at the finish line. The panic of planning a hard launch for my first novel had me paralyzed into doing nothing. Then I discovered the soft launch approach. It's for all these same reasons that I avoid pre-orders like the plague."

Emma Lombard

"I worry I don't know enough, that I'm doing something 'wrong.' There are almost too many people out there telling new authors like me 'how to', and I find myself getting lost in the weeds."

F. Lynn Whyte

Appendix 2: More tips on how to be a relaxed author

There were many valuable insights from authors who responded to our survey, so we have included selected quotes with permission from the authors.

These are in response to the question: **What makes you a relaxed author?**

* * *

"Focusing on the fans and followers I have, not the ones I haven't reached yet. Also, taking the dogs for walks."

Matty Dalrymple

"I meditate and visualize daily to calm my nervous system and keep me focused on creating the career and lifestyle I desire. I also take nature walks as often as I can because they help me achieve and maintain mindfulness."

Robin Lehman

"My workcations. I love going away for 2-3 days in a beautiful setting and giving myself permission to work on my books and nothing else. I work in a hyper-focused way that still feels relaxing because it's what I'm there to do."

Holly Worton

"1. Walks in the forest.

2. Keeping track of how much time I get to write — it usually ends up being more than I realized, which makes me feel positive.

3. Spending time with fellow creatives, especially authors. Whether we write, talk about writing, or just talk about writing, I always feel better afterwards. I'm an introvert, so I don't usually do this in groups bigger than about 3 or 4.

4. Writing in my writing journal. I like to write my thoughts on movies, shows, or books — what worked and what didn't. I like to write about 'where I am right now.' I also write about my stories when I'm stuck."

Jennifer Roundell

"Focusing on my goals and what I like to write. Remembering that the joy comes from the writing, which is completely under my control. Experiencing the mystical creative process, collaborating with God/the Universe/Choose Your Term, is what's most important (to me) and the ultimate anxiety antidote."

Sarah Ettritch

"Therapy. Uninterrupted time. A calming space. Making time to read books I enjoy. Being spiritual. Having other author friends and a weekly critique group."

Danielle Mathieson Pederson

"Something I've recently started doing that has made a huge difference is intentionally celebrating the small successes. When I publish something, I buy a 250ml bottle of champagne and make a fancy dinner for my family. I share what I've done and everyone tells me how clever I am and we toast my success. It's not just a good boost for my ego, but it affirms that I'm working hard and that each book is a step toward my goal of a full-time writing income. I'm celebrating the process, not the results.

I'm really glad I didn't wait to celebrate the result. My grandma died last year, but we had a dinner celebrating the last book I published with her. She told me how proud she was of me, and I know how much she supported me. If I had waited until I'd hit my income goal to celebrate, I would not have that memory with her. Don't wait. Celebrate now."

Gillian St. Kevern

"I focus on why I write. I have a strong career income and am building my writing business to provide creative outlet and income in retirement years. When writing becomes a chore, another pressure job, then I step back. Also, daily meditation, weight lifting, eating well, sleeping 8 hours a night, and avoiding social media FOMO."

Dave Bartell

"Take the long view. It's far more productive to have a strong backlist that will thrill the reader who's just found you for the first time than to bash your skull in trying to claw new readers out of the shadows for your one title."

Lars D. H. Hedbor

"I love doing it my own way. I don't do Facebook or AMS ads. I don't rapid release. I write what I love. I focus on what I enjoy, and it has made all the difference for me."

Sarra Cannon

"Reframing my perspective from one of significance to one of lightness. I've recently made a decision to write for myself and not for profit; though profit would be nice, it's not a 'have to.'"

Anonymous

"Tuning out more and more of the above chatter, or in other words: giving myself permission to be a… well, a happy mid-high five-figure author. That's more than enough, right? Reminding myself that I've had a career for ten years and I've done none of the things on that list. And I strongly suspect that I wouldn't still be here a decade later, happily writing, if I hadn't ignored most of this stuff and gone on doing things my own way."

Charlotte E. English

"When I started to embrace my constitution as a creative, an author and an Asperger, things were set into another light. I started to see that it's okay to not have all the answers. And it's okay to follow my inner drive and passions rather than doing what others want me to do (I did that for 40 years, resulting in severe health issues). So now, when I feel the inner urge to work on my fantasy series (currently in world-building phase), I'll stop everything else and do it."

Anonymous

"Blocking out time for writing. A daily walk helps to keep things in perspective, give me time to organize priorities, and de-stress."

Mark Probert

"1. Paying an assistant to do all the admin stuff

2. Nobody will remember when your book comes out, only whether they liked it or not. So take your time.

3. All deadlines are self-imposed and therefore mutable.

4. Keep a folder of 'puffs,' praise, positive reviews, 'this book changed my life,' etc. When coming across a bad review, dilute its effect by reading the puffs.

5. If your core readership loves the book, it doesn't matter a damn if others don't.

6. Time off is necessary. I usually get my best ideas and most productive days right after mooching about doing nothing for a while. Embrace the slow times.

7. Sometimes what you need to do is write rubbish that will be deleted, or indeed stare at a blank page for a while. It's all part of the process."

Guy Windsor

"Having a schedule and being able to stick with it helps keep the panic at bay."

Linda Shenton Matchett

"Being an indie author is so much 'bigger' than I expected. There are so many tasks, so many options, so many decisions. It's important to keep my focus on the joy I find in the best parts of this journey (and there are lots of best parts!)."

Jemi Fraser

"Moderate exercise and daily centering meditation help everything in my life.

Another thing that helps me relax is to remember that my business is my business. I have a list of the many things I need to take care of both as an author and a publisher. It's only me that says they all need to be done at once, so I can also decide that I'll get to these tasks when I have the time and energy. No one else is looking at my business and judging me. No one knows that my IP tracking is behind, or that my website needs updating but me. And if the next book is taking longer to finish than I want? No one really knows that, either.

Alerts on my phone calendar for regular task scheduling means I'm not keeping it all in my head, stressed about remembering what needs doing.

In the writing business, storytelling always comes first. Connection is second. Everything else is whipped cream on the cake."

T. Thorn Coyle

"I find the best way to relax in this business is to do all of the planning and figuring out ahead of time, so I know what needs to be done and how long I have to do it before I need to worry. In retrospect, I also wish I would stop putting things on pre-order before the first draft is done!"

Amanda Lynn Petrin

"Actually writing. When I get in the zone, I'm in another world, and it's amazing."

Anonymous

"I am most relaxed when I just write, get lost in my story, getting the words down, and walking away from a writing session almost punch drunk on the euphoria of being creative on the page."

Janna Roznos

"Going for a walk when either stumped or unsure of myself. And listening to podcasts that tell me I will be fine (I guess knowing that most authors feel the same!)"

Beth Farrar

"Because I have a paid job (outside of writing) I can go at my own pace without pressure to release the next book quickly. I realize it's okay to make mistakes and learn from them (I'm learning all the time)."

Anonymous

"Being organized. If I have a plan, write lists, and focus then things are way more relaxed and cohesive. Unfortunately, I'm also a slow learner and haven't quite achieved this consistently yet."

Wendy Vella

"Dial back the emotion by recognizing that your books are not your 'babies,' they're your IP (intellectual property.) Do your best and then step back."

Anonymous

"Taking play time. Reading. Choosing to write stories that are great fun. Trusting my Writing Brain and my storytelling abilities. Having cheerleaders, exchanging friendly feedback with other authors (because they understand storytelling tricks). Supportive peer groups."

Hannah Steenbock

"I think you have to make friends with your muse (who is real, and is another word for your roiling subconscious). I think you have to give yourself permission to believe that it is possible you are about to write the best words ever in any writing session. And that you have to banish or cage the probability demons (which are screaming that you're going to write crap, that you would be better off cleaning out the drainpipe, etc.). Probability is a downer. Possibility is the wind beneath your wings. Or the oil in your creative engine."

Kelly McClymer

"I relax most while I'm writing. When the words flow and my fingers fly over the keyboard, that makes me happy and relaxed. I can shut out real life and live in my make-believe world for a few hours a day. This allows me to come back into reality and deal with everything going on around me."

Deanna L. Rowley

"Get rid of pre-order deadlines."

Pamela Kelley

"When I'm drafting, I write only for myself. I'm the only audience. The only goal is for me to write about something that interests me, to discover what I think about a topic or create a world or characters that I want to spend time with. Drafting on paper (nice paper, with nice pens!) also makes writing feel more relaxed and luxurious rather than 'work,' which I associate more with the computer."

Kristen Tate

"Knowing that my life isn't over if I fail at being a writer. I'd be disappointed, of course, but I have enough income coming in that I don't have to succeed to keep my family fed. That takes a huge load off my mind."

ChemistKen

"Please recognize that for some people, work IS relaxing. I'm happiest when I'm working. So if I absolutely MUST relax (usually because my family or my health demands I take time off), I need to schedule that in and make it a to-do list item. Having random free time stresses me out more than it relaxes me. It's just the way my brain works. So for people like me (high in that Achiever strength in the Clifton Strengths), I recommend adding it into the routine (read during your lunch break instead of working, for example), and adding relaxing things to the to-do lists."

Liza Street

"Small walks. Whenever I'm overly stressing over writing, formatting, or any of it, taking a short walk helps me immensely."

Leigh Badger

"Hiking is one of the best ways for me to fill my reserves and relax. I'll even put on forest sounds during writing sessions or at work."

Jana M Floyd

"Focusing on building a sustainable business for the long term: which means making great books, collecting my own customers (e.g. through a mailing list) and building a foundation to eventually sell more products in more places, and especially direct to customers!"

D.J. Jacobson

"Focusing on the craft and refusing to attach my self-worth as an author to either sales or reviews. I got into this business to create and although, yes, it's important to pay my bills, stressing over how many books I sell isn't going to help me shift an increasing number, anymore than stressing over a bad review will change the reviewers perspective on my work. The bottom line is: stress doesn't change anything, except your mood and productivity. For the worse."

Helen Cox

"Talk to other writers! I'm part of a very small chat group made up of successful authors in my genre and we share our fears, doubts and wins with each other. It feels so good to have people who understand you!"

Sophie-Leigh Robbins

"When I can talk with other writers, talk about my story, it takes me a lot to get over my anxiety and introvert fear. Seeing how generous and helpful more experienced authors can be gives me hope and helps me understand that as I put in time and effort, my skills will naturally improve and hopefully my confidence, too. Then I can see myself becoming more relaxed."

F. Lynn Whyte

"Routines help me. Knowing exactly what I'll start my writing day with, what will be second, etc., instead of reinventing the wheel each time I sit to write really helps. Also, setting low, reasonable goals. For example, my word count goal used to be 2,000 per day, which was great when I did NaNo, but in my regular life it's hard to attain. I've lowered it to 500 per day, and it's so much easier to make the mark. Also, I congratulate myself if I get 100 words in a day, trying not to break the streak. I figure if I write 500 words every day, on average, I can produce three books per year, and I can live with that."

Tiffany Dickinson

Appendix 3: Resources by chapter

1.3 Write in a series (if you want to)

- Interview with fantasy author Lindsay Buroker on writing a series — www.TheCreativePenn.com/writeseries
- *How to Write a Series* — Sara Rosett

1.4 Schedule time to fill the creative well and for rest and relaxation

- The Ultimate Guide to Creative Rest for Indie Authors — www.selfpublishingadvice.org/the-ultimate-guide-to-creative-rest-for-indie-authors

2.1 Make empowered publishing choices that suit your personality and your life. Re-evaluate over time.

- *Successful Self-Publishing: How to Self-Publish and Market Your Book* — Joanna Penn

- *Wide for the Win: Strategies to Sell Globally via Multiple Platforms and For Your Own Path to Success* — Mark Leslie Lefebvre

- *Killing It On Kobo: Leverage Insights to Optimize Publishing and Marketing Strategies: Grow Your Global Sales and Increase Revenue on Kobo*
  — Mark Leslie Lefebvre

2.2 Understand persistence, patience and partnership if traditionally publishing

- *The 7 P's of Publishing Success*
  — Mark Leslie Lefebvre

- *Publishing Pitfalls for Authors*
  — Mark Leslie Lefebvre

- *Closing the Deal… On Your Terms: Agents, Contracts, and Other Considerations*
  — Kristine Kathryn Rusch

- Stark Reflections on Writing and Publishing Podcast. Episode 145. Robert J. Sawyer on Leveraging Your IP and Hybrid Publishing — www.starkreflections.ca/robertjsawyer

2.3 Value your work. You create intellectual property assets. Retain control as much as possible.

- *The Copyright Handbook: What Every Writer Needs To Know* — Stephen Fishman
- *Rethinking the Writing Business* — Kristine Kathryn Rusch
- *Selective Rights Licensing: Sell Your Book Rights At Home and Abroad* — Orna A. Ross and Helen Sedwick
- *The Magic Bakery: Copyright in the Modern World of Fiction Publishing* — Dean Wesley Smith
- *Closing the Deal … on Your Terms: Agents, Contracts and Other Considerations* — Kristine Kathryn Rusch
- *How To Make a Living With Your Writing: Turn Your Words Into Multiple Streams of Income* — Joanna Penn

- *Hollywood vs. the Author*
  — Edited by Stephen Jay Schwartz

- NFTs for Authors
  — www.TheCreativePenn.com/nfts

- Empowering authors around copyright. Interview with Rebecca Giblin
  — TheCreativePenn.com/rebeccagiblin

- The importance of editing and why authors need to understand their publishing contracts with Ruth Ware
  — www.TheCreativePenn.com/ruthware

- The Society of Authors (UK)
  — SocietyOfAuthors.org

- The Authors Guild (USA)
  — AuthorsGuild.org

- The Alliance of Independent Authors (global)
  — AllianceIndependentAuthors.org

- Pottermore sales and profits rise with 'strong' Harry Potter sales. The Bookseller, Jan 14, 2021 — www.thebookseller.com/news/pottermore-sales-and-profits-rise-strong-harry-potter-sales-1232915

- Stark Reflections on Writing and Publishing Podcast. Episode 105. Location Based Storytelling with Voicemap — www.starkreflections.ca/tag/voicemap/

2.4 Publish at your own pace

- *Publishing Pitfalls for Authors* — Mark Leslie Lefebvre

2.5 Publish wide (or don't)

- *Wide for the Win: Strategies to Sell Globally via Multiple Platforms and for Your Own Path to Success* — Mark Leslie Lefebvre

- *Release Strategies: Plan Your Self-Publishing Schedule for Maximum Benefit* — Craig Martelle and Michael Anderle

- Facebook group Wide For The Win — www.Facebook.com/groups/wideforthewin

- Facebook group 20 Books to 50K — www.Facebook.com/groups/20booksto50k

2.6 Sell direct to your audience

- Payhip for selling ebooks and audiobooks direct — www.TheCreativePenn.com/payhip

- Buy ebooks and audiobooks directly from Joanna — www.Payhip.com/thecreativepenn

- Process of using a Payhip coupon — www.TheCreativePenn.com/payhip-coupon

- Bookfunnel for delivery of ebooks and audiobooks — www.TheCreativePenn.com/bookfunnel

- Joanna's tutorial on selling ebooks and audiobooks direct with Payhip and Bookfunnel — www.TheCreativePenn.com/selldirecttutorial

- The Ultimate Guide to Selling Books on your Author Website by the Alliance of Independent Authors — SelfPublishingAdvice.org/selling-books-on-your-author-website

- NFTs for Authors — www.TheCreativePenn.com/nfts

2.7 Don't let piracy and plagiarism derail you

- The Indie Author's Guide to Managing Piracy by the Alliance of Independent Authors — www.SelfPublishingAdvice.org/indie-authors-guide-to-managing-piracy

- The Indie Author Guide to Managing Plagiarism by the Alliance of Independent Authors — www.SelfPublishingAdvice.org/is-copyright-broken-part-2-the-indie-authors-guide-to-managing-plagiarism

- If you want to check your own work in case you have inadvertently plagiarized someone, you can use tools like ProWritingAid — www.TheCreativePenn.com/prowritingaid

- Nora Roberts files 'multi-plagiarism' lawsuit alleging writer copied more than 40 authors. The Guardian, 25 April 2019 — www.theguardian.com/books/2019/apr/25/nora-roberts-files-multi-plagiarism-lawsuit-alleging-writer-copied-more-than-40-authors

- Insights from the Immersive Media & Books 2020 Consumer Survey. Stark Reflections Podcast Episode 147 — www.starkreflections.ca/2021/05/14/episode-191-insights-from-the-immersive-media-books-2020-consumer-survey/

- Immersive Media & Books 2020 Consumer Survey, via Panorama Project — www.panoramaproject.org/immersive-media-reading-2020

2.8 Deal with cancel culture, bad reviews and haters

- *The Successful Author Mindset: A Handbook for Surviving the Writer's Journey*
  — Joanna Penn

- *Resilience: Facing Down Rejection and Criticism on the Road to Success*
  — Mark McGuinness

2.9 Find a community who support your publishing choices

- Alliance of Independent Authors
  — www.allianceindependentauthors.org

- *Networking for Authors* — Dan Parsons

- Interview on Networking for Authors with Dan Parsons
  — www.TheCreativePenn.com/networking

- Facebook group Wide for the Win
  — www.facebook.com/groups/wideforthewin

- Facebook group 20BooksTo50K
  — www.facebook.com/groups/20Booksto50k

3.1 Focus on the basics first

- *Successful Self-Publishing: How to Self-Publish and Market Your Book* — Joanna Penn
- *Wide for the Win: Strategies to Sell Globally via Multiple Platforms and for Your Own Path to Success* — Mark Leslie Lefebvre
- *How to Market a Book* — Joanna Penn
- *How to Market a Book: Over Perform in a Crowded Market* — Ricardo Fayet
- Publisher Rocket. Tool for Categories and Keywords: www.TheCreativePenn.com/rocket
- K-Lytics. Research for specific Amazon categories: www.TheCreativePenn.com/genre
- List of book cover designers and a tutorial on how to find and work with cover designers: www.TheCreativePenn.com/bookcoverdesign

3.3 Simplify and automate your email

- Tutorial on how to set up your email list with ConvertKit — www.TheCreativePenn.com/setup-email-list
- *Newsletter Ninja: How to Become an Author Mailing List Expert* — Tammi Labrecque

3.4 Find one form of marketing that you enjoy and can sustain for the long term

- *Audio for Authors: Audiobooks, Podcasting, and Voice Technologies* — Joanna Penn
- The Creative Penn Podcast — www.TheCreativePenn.com/podcast
- Books and Travel Podcast — www.BooksAndTravel.page/listen
- Stark Reflections on Writing and Publishing — www.StarkReflections.ca

3.5 Put book 1 in a series free or permafree and schedule regular promotions

- *BookBub Ads Expert: A Marketing Guide to Author Discovery* — David Gaughran
- Freebooksy is just one of the paid promotional newsletter options at WrittenWordMedia.com

3.8 Outsource when you can

- Reedsy marketplace for freelancers who work specifically with authors — www.TheCreativePenn.com/reedsy

- Upwork marketplace for freelancers — www.Upwork.com

- *Productivity for Authors: Find Time to Write, Organize Your Author Life and Decide What Really Matters* — Joanna Penn

- Getting a Creative Edge with Publicist Mickey Mikkelson. Stark Reflections on Writing and Publishing Episode 163 — www.starkreflections.ca/2020/11/20/episode-163-getting-a-creative-edge-with-mickey-mikkelson/

4.1 Do you really want to run an author business?

- *Your Author Business Plan: Take Your Author Career to The Next Level* — Joanna Penn

- *Business for Authors: How to be an Author Entrepreneur* — Joanna Penn

- *Big Magic: Creative Living Beyond Fear* — Elizabeth Gilbert

4.2 Create multiple streams of income

- *How to Make A Living With Your Writing: Turn Your Words Into Multiple Streams of Income* — Joanna Penn

- Winning as a Hybrid Author. Interview with Kevin J. Anderson. Episode 24 of Draft2Digital's Self-Publishing Insiders Podcast — www.draft2digital.com/blog/winning-as-a-hybrid-author-with-kevin-j-anderson-self-publishing-insiders-ep024/

4.3 Eliminate tasks. Say 'no' more

- *Anything You Want: 40 Lessons for a New Kind of Entrepreneur* — Derek Sivers

- *Productivity for Authors: Find Time To Write, Organize Your Author Life, and Decide What Really Matters* — Joanna Penn

4.4 Organize and improve your processes

- *Productivity for Authors: Find Time To Write, Organize Your Author Life, and Decide What Really Matters* — Joanna Penn

- *Deep Work: Rules For Focused Success in a Distracted World* — Cal Newport

4.5 Use tools to make your process more efficient and save time and money

- List of tools and tutorials for writers by Joanna Penn
  — www.TheCreativePenn.com/tools

- Scrivener for writing and plotting/organizing
  www.TheCreativePenn.com/scrivenersoftware

- ProWritingAid for editing
  — www.TheCreativePenn.com/prowritingaid

- Vellum for ebook and print formatting
  — www.TheCreativePenn.com/vellum

- Publisher Rocket
  — www.TheCreativePenn.com/rocket

- Buffer social media scheduling
  — www.buffer.com

- Canva image creation — www.canva.com

- Bookfunnel for delivery of ebooks and audiobooks — www.Bookfunnel.com

- Payhip for direct sales — www.Payhip.com

- ConvertKit for email management — www.TheCreativePenn.com/convert

- Example FAQ page — www.TheCreativePenn.com/faq

- Example form for email — www.TheCreativePenn.com/contact

- There are lots of forms you can use depending on your website. Joanna uses Gravity Forms — www.gravityforms.com

- Calendly for scheduling — www.calendly.com

- Xero for invoicing and accounting — www.xero.com

- ScribeCount — www.markleslie.ca/scribecount

- Headliner for audio sharing — www.headliner.app

- BookBrush for book ads — www.BookBrush.com

- Universal Book Links — www.Books2Read.com

- Draft2Digital payment splitting — www.draft2digital.com/blog/announcing-d2d-payment-splitting/

- 32 Best Free Backup Software Tools: Reviews of the best free backup software for Windows. *LiveWire*, July 1, 2021 — www.lifewire.com/free-backup-software-tools-2617964

4.6 Find voices you trust and tune out the rest

- *On Writing: A Memoir of the Craft* — Stephen King

- Books for authors by Dean Wesley Smith and Kristine Kathryn Rusch — www.wmgpublishinginc.com/writers/

- Kris Rusch's Business articles on Patreon — Patreon.com/kristinekathrynrusch

4.7 Learn about money

- List of recommended money books and podcasts — www.TheCreativePenn.com/moneybooks

- Joanna Penn on the Choose FI Podcast — www.ChooseFI.com/the-creative-penn/

- *The Wealthy Barber: Everyone's Common Sense Guide to Becoming Financially Independent* — David Chilton

4.8 Look after your physical and mental health

- *The Healthy Writer: Reduce Your Pain, Improve Your Health, and Build a Writing Career for the Long Term* — Joanna Penn and Dr Euan Lawson

- *Fast, Feast, Repeat: The Comprehensive Guide to Delay, Don't Deny Intermittent Fasting* — Gin Stephens

- Intermittent Fasting Stories Podcast with Gin Stephens. Episode 155 is with Joanna Penn. On your favorite podcast app or www.intermittentfastingstories.com

4.9 Keep a long-term mindset

- *The Successful Author Mindset: A Handbook for Surviving the Writer's Journey* — Joanna Penn

- *The 7 P's of Publishing Success* — Mark Leslie Lefebvre

Appendix 4: Bibliography

Anything You Want: 40 Lessons for a New Kind of Entrepreneur — Derek Sivers

Audio for Authors: Audiobooks, Podcasting, and Voice Technologies — Joanna Penn

Big Magic: Creative Living Beyond Fear — Elizabeth Gilbert

BookBub Ads Expert: A Marketing Guide to Author Discovery — David Gaughran

Business for Authors: How to be an Author Entrepreneur — Joanna Penn

Closing the Deal… On Your Terms: Agents, Contracts, and Other Considerations — Kristine Kathryn Rusch

Deep Work: Rules For Focused Success in a Distracted World — Cal Newport

Fast, Feast, Repeat: The Comprehensive Guide to Delay, Don't Deny Intermittent Fasting
— Gin Stephens

Hollywood vs. the Author
— Edited by Stephen Jay Schwartz

How to Make a Living With Your Writing: Turn Your Words Into Multiple Streams of Income
— Joanna Penn

How to Market a Book — Joanna Penn

How to Market a Book: Over Perform in a Crowded Market — Ricardo Fayet

How to Write a Series — Sara Rosett

Killing It On Kobo: Leverage Insights to Optimize Publishing and Marketing Strategies: Grow Your Global Sales and Increase Revenue on Kobo — Mark Leslie Lefebvre

Networking for Authors — Dan Parsons

Newsletter Ninja: How to Become an Author Mailing List Expert — Tammi Labrecque

On Writing: A Memoir of the Craft
— Stephen King

Productivity for Authors: Find Time to Write, Organize Your Author Life and Decide What Really Matters — Joanna Penn

Publishing Pitfalls for Authors — Mark Leslie Lefebvre

Release Strategies: Plan Your Self-Publishing Schedule for Maximum Benefit — Craig Martelle and Michael Anderle

Resilience: Facing Down Rejection and Criticism on the Road to Success — Mark McGuinness

Rethinking the Writing Business — Kristine Kathryn Rusch

Selective Rights Licensing: Sell Your Book Rights at Home and Abroad — Orna A. Ross and Helen Sedwick

Successful Self-Publishing: How to Self-Publish and Market Your Book — Joanna Penn

The 7 P's of Publishing Success — Mark Leslie Lefebvre

The Copyright Handbook: What Every Writer Needs To Know — Stephen Fishman

The Healthy Writer: Reduce Your Pain, Improve Your Health, and Build a Writing Career for the Long Term — Joanna Penn and Dr Euan Lawson

The Magic Bakery: Copyright in the Modern World of Fiction Publishing — Dean Wesley Smith

The Successful Author Mindset: A Handbook for Surviving The Writer's Journey — Joanna Penn

The Wealthy Barber: Everyone's Common Sense Guide to Becoming Financially Independent — David Chilton

Wide for the Win: Strategies to Sell Globally via Multiple Platforms and For Your Own Path to Success — Mark Leslie Lefebvre

Your Author Business Plan: Take Your Author Career to the Next Level — Joanna Penn

More Books and Courses from Joanna Penn

Non-Fiction Books for Authors

How to Write Non-Fiction

How to Market a Book

How to Make a Living with your Writing

Productivity for Authors

Successful Self-Publishing

Your Author Business Plan

The Successful Author Mindset

Public Speaking for Authors, Creatives and Other Introverts

Audio for Authors: Audiobooks, Podcasting, and Voice Technologies

The Healthy Writer

Business for Authors:

How to be an Author Entrepreneur

Co-writing a Book

Career Change

www.TheCreativePenn.com/books

Courses for authors

How to Write a Novel

How to Write Non-Fiction

Multiple Streams of Income from your Writing

Your Author Business Plan

Content Marketing for Fiction

Productivity for Authors

Turn What You Know Into An Online Course

www.TheCreativePenn.com/courses

Thriller novels as J.F. Penn

ARKANE Action-adventure Thrillers

Stone of Fire #1
Crypt of Bone #2
Ark of Blood #3
One Day In Budapest #4

Day of the Vikings #5
Gates of Hell #6
One Day in New York #7
Destroyer of Worlds #8
End of Days #9
Valley of Dry Bones #10
Tree of Life #11
Tomb of Relics #12

Brooke and Daniel Crime Thrillers

Desecration #1
Delirium #2
Deviance #3

Mapwalker Dark Fantasy Trilogy

Map of Shadows #1
Map of Plagues #2
Map of the Impossible #3

Other Books and Short Stories

Risen Gods

A Thousand Fiendish Angels:
Short stories based on Dante's Inferno

The Dark Queen:
An Underwater Archaeology Short Story

More books coming soon.

You can sign up to be notified
of new releases, giveaways and pre-release
specials - plus, get a free book!

www.JFPenn.com/free

More Books from Mark Leslie Lefebvre

Stark Publishing Solutions

The 7 P's of Publishing Success

Killing It on Kobo

An Author's Guide to Working with Libraries and Bookstores

Wide for the Win

Publishing Pitfalls for Authors

Co-authored titles

Taking the Short Tack: Creating Income and Connecting with Readers using Short Fiction — with Matty Dalrymple

The Relaxed Author: Take the Pressure off Your Art and Enjoy the Creative Journey — with Joanna Penn

Under Mark Leslie

Canadian Werewolf

This Time Around (Short Story—Free) #0

A Canadian Werewolf in New York #1

Stowe Away (Novella) #1.5

Fear and Longing in Los Angeles #2

Fright Nights, Big City #3

Other Novels

Evasion

I, Death

Short Fiction Collections

One Hand Screaming

Nocturnal Screams

Snowman Shivers: Dark Humor Snowman Tales

Bumps in the Night: Creepy Campfire Tales

Tricky Treats: Three Halloween Tales

Nobody's Hero

Non-Fiction Ghost Stories & Paranormal

Haunted Hamilton: The Ghosts of Dundurn Castle and Other Steeltown Shivers

Spooky Sudbury: True Tales of the Eerie & Supernatural — with Jenny Jelen

Tomes of Terror: Haunted Bookstores and Libraries

Creepy Capital: Ghost Stories of Ottawa and the National Capital Region

Haunted Hospitals: Eerie Tales about Hospitals, Sanatoriums and Other Institutions — with Rhonda Parrish

Macabre Montreal: Ghostly Tales, Ghastly Events, and Gruesome True Stories — with Shayna Krishnasamy

Too Macabre for Montreal: Tales Deemed Too Disturbing for Macabre Montreal — with Shayna Krishnasamy

Anthology Editor

North of Infinity II

Campus Chills

Tesseracts Sixteen: *Parnassus Unbound*

Fiction River: Editor's Choice

Fiction River: Feel the Fear

Fiction River: Feel the Love

Fiction River: Superstitious

Obsessions

Pulphouse Fiction Magazine 10

About Joanna Penn

Joanna Penn writes non-fiction for authors and is an award-nominated, New York Times and USA Today bestselling thriller author as J.F. Penn. She's also an award-winning podcaster, creative entrepreneur, and international professional speaker.

She is an international professional speaker, podcaster, and award-winning entrepreneur. She lives in Bath, England with her husband and enjoys a nice G&T.

Joanna's award-winning site for writers, TheCreativePenn.com, helps people to write, publish and market their books through articles, audio, video and online products as well as live workshops.

Love thrillers? www.JFPenn.com

Love travel? Check out my Books and Travel podcast www.BooksAndTravel.page

Connect with Joanna

www.TheCreativePenn.com
joanna@TheCreativePenn.com

www.twitter.com/thecreativepenn
www.facebook.com/TheCreativePenn
www.Instagram.com/jfpennauthor
www.youtube.com/thecreativepenn

About Mark Leslie Lefebvre

Mark's highly successful experience in the publishing and bookselling industry spans four decades where he has worked in almost every type of brick-and-mortar, online and digital bookstore and also held the role of President of the Canadian Booksellers Association.

As the former Director of self-publishing and author relations for Rakuten Kobo, the founding leader of Kobo Writing Life, and the consulting Director of Business Development for Draft2Digital, Mark thrives on innovation, particularly as it relates to digital publishing. He was part of the Professional Advisory Committee for the establishment of Sheridan College's Writing and Publishing Program, and guest lectures about the business of writing and publishing at numerous other university and college programs.

A professional speaker who has given talks throughout North America, the UK, and Europe, Mark also writes and mentors authors and publishers about digital publishing opportunities both 1:1 and via his Stark Reflections on Writing & Publishing weekly podcast.

You can learn more about Mark at www.markleslie.ca

Acknowledgments

From Joanna: Thanks to my community and patrons at The Creative Penn website and podcast. Your enthusiasm and support keeps me going!

From Mark: Thank you to the awesome listeners of The Creative Penn podcast who first suggested this book after hearing Joanna and me joking about it in an episode. And also, giant hugs to listeners and patrons of the Stark Reflections on Writing and Publishing podcast who also support and propel me forward on this and so many other projects. I love you guys.

Thanks to the 200 writers who took our Relaxed Author survey in June 2021 and thanks in particular to the authors quoted within the book.

Thanks to Jane Dixon Smith for the cover design and print interior formatting, and to Liz Dexter at LibroEditing for proofreading.

www.ingramcontent.com/pod-product-compliance
Lightning Source LLC
Chambersburg PA
CBHW071725080526
44588CB00013B/1901